EDUCATIONAL TECHNOLOGY

BEST PRACTICES FROM AMERICA'S SCHOOLS

Second Edition

William Bozeman

University of Central Florida

EYE ON EDUCATION
6 DEPOT WAY WEST, SUITE 106
LARCHMONT, NY 10538
(914) 833–0551
(914) 833–0761 fax

Library of Congress Cataloging-in-Publication Data

Bozeman, William C.
    Educational technology : best practices from America's schools / William C. Bozeman. -- 2nd ed.
        p.   cm.
    Includes bibliographical references and indexes.
    ISBN 1-883001-59-5
    1. Educational technology—United States—Case studies.
2. Educational innovations—United States—Case studies.
    3. Educational surveys—United States.   I. Title.
LB1028.3.B59   1999
371.33—dc21   98–20704
                                                                        CIP

10 9 8 7 6 5 4 3 2

Editorial and production services provided by Richard H. Adin Freelance Editorial Services, 9 Orchard Drive, Gardiner, NY 12525 (914-883-5884)

Also Available from EYE ON EDUCATION

**The Educator's Brief Guide to the Internet
and the World Wide Web**
by Eugene F. Provenzo, Jr.

The Educator's Brief Guide to Computers in the Schools
by Eugene F. Provenzo, Jr.

The Principal as Steward
by Jack McCall

The Principal's Edge
by Jack McCall

**Performance Assessment and Standards-Based Curricula:
The Achievement Cycle**
by Allan A. Glatthorn with Don Bragaw,
Karen Dawkins, and John Parker

Research on Educational Innovations, 2d ed.
by Arthur K. Ellis and Jeffrey T. Fouts

Research on School Restructuring
by Arthur K. Ellis and Jeffrey T. Fouts

Handbook of Educational Terms and Applications
by Arthur K. Ellis and Jeffrey T. Fouts

Teaching in the Block
by Robert Lynn Canady and Michael D. Rettig

Block Scheduling
by Robert Lynn Canady and Michael D. Rettig

The Administrator's Guide to School-Community Relations
by George E. Pawlas

Innovations in Parent and Family Involvement
by William Rioux and Nancy Berla

**The Reflective Supervisor:
A Practical Guide for Educators**
by Ray Calabrese and Sally Zepeda

ACKNOWLEDGEMENTS

The anxiety of authors is always high when preparing this section. So many individuals contribute to the products of one's work. Acknowledgements are also a pleasure to write because they represent one of those rare occasions where one can formally express appreciation for contributions and assistance. I hope this effort will bring some measure of pride to those persons. Among those who contributed their time were Christie Adams, Ann Barron, John Cullum, Lori Hiatt, and Stephanie Soliven. I also wish to thank my publisher Bob Sickles for his support.

This book is dedicated to all those wonderful educators who have embraced instructional technology in their schools and classrooms. Our work has just begun.

This work is also dedicated to my parents who believed in the power of education.

ABOUT THE AUTHOR

William Bozeman received his Ph.D. from the University of Wisconsin–Madison and currently serves as Professor of Educational Leadership at the University of Central Florida in Orlando. Prior to joining the faculty at UCF, he was professor and chair at The University of Iowa. His educational background includes experience as a high school principal and mathematics/physics teacher. While a graduate student at Madison, Dr. Bozeman served as a Project Associate with the Wisconsin Research and Development Center. In addition to experiences in education, he has worked and consulted extensively in the areas of systems planning and design, educational technology, and program evaluation. Dr. Bozeman has published extensively in the areas of education, educational technology, and systems planning and design, including three books. He also served as coeditor of *the Journal of Research on Computing in Education* and coauthored the first edition of *Educational Technology: Best Practices From America's Schools*. A former professional musician, Dr. Bozeman enjoys playing guitar, keyboards, and music synthesizers, collecting vintage guitars, and restoring a 1967 Mustang convertible.

TABLE OF CONTENTS

1

INTRODUCTION

Educators continue to be challenged with many complex decision situations—violence, substance abuse, equity issues, multicultural education, values, bilingual education, choice, declining test scores, tight budgets—and these are just some of the challenges facing educators today. A possible solution in many of these problematic areas is educational technology. Yet, technology continues to be elusive and just beyond the reach of some schools and school districts. This is disappointing, given that educational technology applications have been evident for over three decades and have grown at an especially rapid rate during the decade of the 1990s. The good news is that there is indeed a flurry of activity in the nation's schools that reflects innovative and productive growth in technology applications. *Educational Technology: Best Practices from America's Schools* offers a glimpse of these projects and, hopefully, will encourage educators to pursue an investigation and application of these and other good programs.

Since the first edition of *Educational Technology: Best Practices from America's Schools*, much advancement has been made in educational technology, especially in computers and computer-related hardware. It is likely that this technological progress, and accompanying declines in costs, will lead to many changes and improvements in instructional technology. In fact, it may be argued that we are only beginning to realize the real promises of educational technology.

A recent survey by *T.H.E. Journal* reported another upward growth in educational technology buying trends. Approximately 11 billion dollars was spent in 1997 by education for technology-related products in the United States. This expenditure makes educational institutions one of the single largest purchasers of hardware, software, peripherals, and support services in the United States. *T.H.E. Journal*'s survey also revealed several interesting market shifts. Apple Macintosh is declining in sales in both K-12 and in higher education (although Apple is the largest installed computer platform in education). Integrated Learning Systems (ILS) purchases declined for a third straight year. Networking products were the top priority purchase in 1997. Interest in distance learning and online connections made telecommunications products a high priority also. These figures do not include student-purchased or faculty-purchased computers. Compare this scenario with the mid-1980s when only about two million microcomputer units were installed in educational institutions.

Expenditures for faculty and staff development are a bit more elusive. This area continues to be problematic, both at the teacher pre-service level in colleges of education and the in-service support provided by schools and districts. Most educators continue to perceive pre-service technology education to be lacking in scope or substance. When educational leaders place computers in classrooms and offer unprepared teachers an occasional workshop, effective integration cannot be expected. Yet, this remains the case in too many schools. Research and experience continue to demonstrate that certain key components are essential to successful technology applications: administrative support, adequate training, ready access to hardware and software, technical support, and appropriate curriculum planning. In this regard, the role of technology in educational change and improvement must be considered from a total systems perspective.

Educators still express reservations about the utility of educational technology and are cautious and conservative when decisions must be made. Opinions are mixed as to the real benefits accrued through instructional technology. Why is this the case? Why do many, if not most, professionals outside education consider the computer an absolute necessity? Why are American schools behind business, industry, and the military in their use of technology? This is true despite a growing body of evidence that supports the effectiveness of educational technology as an instructional delivery system. It is probably counterproductive to belabor the reasons for their reticence in this work; the reasons are better treated elsewhere. It is important to note, however, that the past decade has witnessed great progress in our nation's schools with regard to technology. Economies of scale in software production, along with significant decreases in hardware costs, have made educational technology affordable for almost any school or district. Careful operational and strategic planning is critical to maintaining this momentum in technology implementation.

As stated before, the issue of faculty and personnel development is paramount. Regrettably, many graduates of today's colleges of education are not prepared to effectively use technology as an instructional delivery system or to integrate technology into their curriculum. While teacher-training institutions retrain their faculty and revamp the curriculum, it is incumbent upon schools, districts, and other educational institutions to also retrain their faculty to integrate technology into their teaching methods. They must also retrain administrators, especially at the building level, to provide the much needed leadership as well as to be accountable for management of technology resources. Indeed, technology is changing the very nature of education. Already, incredible information resources are available at low cost to practically anyone; this accessibility alone can change the way we teach and learn. Once the maxim "Knowledge is power" was accepted without question as a guiding principle. Today, with the myriad of online resources, a more appropriate axiom might be "Ability to access and use knowledge is power." Successful teachers will be able to not only help students access data and information, but also to show them how to connect, synthesize, and integrate this massive resource.

As educators contemplate planning for technology, one of the questions I am frequently asked, in one form or another, is: "What are other schools doing with computer-based educational technology?" This is a reasonable question, because many educational systems are based on replication of successful practices. *Educational Technology: Best Practices from*

America's Schools is a compilation of exemplary programs and projects in elementary and secondary schools throughout the United States. The book is intended for anyone interested in the impact and implications of the emerging technologies in education. It answers two of the most frequently asked questions: "What are other educators doing with technology in their schools and districts?" and "What are some educational technology practices that have demonstrated success?" Faculty members, administrators, students, school board members, and concerned members of a community will find the case studies a valuable resource as they contemplate implementation and integration of educational technologies. Such technologies include computer-based education, distance education, the Internet, multimedia, networks, computer laboratories, telecommunications, interactive video, and the creative use of the computer as an integral instructional tool.

The technology profiles presented here are from several sources, but are primarily the product of a reputational survey and literature review conducted in 1997. Nominations were requested from state departments of education, leaders of professional associations, and other knowledgeable persons in the field. In addition, journals, periodicals, and conference proceedings related to educational technology were reviewed for possible sites. Sites nominated in this first phase of the study were contacted regarding their interest in participation and were provided a survey form. The programs selected for inclusion are considered representative not only of programs worthy of examination pedagogically, but also of programs that may merit replication or that may be transportable to other schools and districts.

Objectives of the text include, but are not limited to, the following:

- To catalog innovative applications of educational technology
- To present information and overviews of the respective applications and the structure of their systems
- To identify how various programs address the educational needs of a school and community

- ◆ To determine the resources (human, financial, and physical) required to implement the respective programs
- ◆ To assist in understanding the obstacles and pitfalls associated with the innovations
- ◆ To facilitate understanding, decision making, and implementation of educational technology programs and practices in other schools and school districts

Each program case study includes the following information:

- ◆ Goals of the program
- ◆ Keywords (descriptors of the program)
- ◆ Location
- ◆ Description of school and community (general demographic information)
- ◆ Description of program
- ◆ Outcomes, results, and accomplishments
- ◆ Difficulties (both anticipated and unanticipated)
- ◆ Things to consider (if replicating a program)
- ◆ Costs (start-up, maintenance, operation) and other resource requirements
- ◆ Contact person(s) for additional information

This information is accurate and current, to the best of the author's knowledge. Survey information was cycled through several iterations along with numerous exchanges with school representatives via telephone, fax, and electronic mail. It is recognized, of course, that technology applications are "moving targets" and the programs are subject to rapid change.

Chapter 2 deals with one of the constant sources of tension among educators—that is, "how much" one needs to understand about the actual, technical operations of computer systems. An overview of fundamentals of computer technology concepts is offered for persons who require this information. Topics addressed include computer system configurations, input devices, output devices, processing and data storage, primary memory, secondary storage, computer communications (telecommunications and networks), and computer software (operating systems, application software, and programming languages).

Chapter 3 discusses instructional computer applications. Topics include a historical perspective on computing, discussions of the various modes of computer-assisted instruction (CAI), computer-managed instruction (CMI), computer-enhanced instruction (CEI), the computer as an instructional tool (application software), LOGO, authoring programs, presentation software, multimedia, videodiscs, and CD-ROM.

Chapter 4 presents the case studies. There are several ways to use the studies. One method is to use the keyword index to access studies of particular interest or those associated with given areas. Another approach is to peruse those studies associated with a given grade level (elementary, middle, or secondary). Because the studies are offered in a succinct format, it may be valuable to review all the applications as they may stimulate your own creative technology solutions for your specific needs. Also offered are discussions of selected keywords, suggested sources of information, and sample technology plans.

Future successes of educational technology initiatives are reliant on the vision of our school leaders, whether they are classroom teachers, administrators, college professors, school board members, business partners, students, or concerned members of the community. Attitudes of these parties will greatly influence these outcomes. Hopefully, the studies presented will positively shape some attitudes toward a belief and commitment that educational technology can make a difference in our schools. Technology can be the "equalizer" that brings both excellence and equity to the classroom. Technology does not recognize the color of students' skin or their social status; technology offers more with each passing year at a lesser cost, while personnel costs continue to rise; and technology is infinitely patient and never tires of a child's mistakes. Together, technology and teachers can provide a learning environment that guarantees the knowledge, skills, wisdom, and the preparation needed for the twenty-first century.

2

COMPUTER TECHNOLOGY CONCEPTS

WHAT DO YOU NEED TO KNOW?

A source of tension for years among educators, as they discuss computers and related technology applications concerns, has been how much one needs to understand about the actual, technical operations of computer systems. There still is no definitive answer. Some individuals may require only a general knowledge about technical considerations, while others may wish to have in-depth knowledge. When contemplating computer literacy, analogies to other areas of technical literacy, such as the automobile, are often made. For instance, most of the public understands how to access the primary functions or accessories of the automobile (lights, air conditioning, heat, radio, cruise control, etc.). They may also have some rudimentary knowledge of how the vehicle functions and how to perform basic service operations such as changing a tire or checking fluid levels. However, most persons cannot tune the engine or rebuild the transmission. This doesn't prevent them from being proficient drivers and enjoying their cars. Why is the computer any different?

An analogy such as the automobile is misleading because of the many complexities and possibilities in the field of computers and information processing technology. Mastery of all or almost all of the accessories in an automobile may require understanding only a few operations. Computers are more sophisticated and there is so much to learn. Even a basic knowledge of computer systems and operations allows one to overcome fears or apprehensions and to become a more productive user. The more one learns about the system, the more possibilities that are offered. However, there are times when some technical insights are an absolute necessity. It would be wonderful if all hardware and software connections and installation were truly "plug and play." That is just not the case. The installation of certain multimedia configurations (such as MIDI) will almost certainly require some delving into the manuals. Most problems are solvable, but not without some basic understanding and conceptual knowledge of the technology.

Technological knowledge of computing and related topics is not gained merely by reading a chapter or participating in a short course. Technical knowledge is also not gained by memorizing terminology, although the field, like others, has developed a unique language. Unfamiliarity with the language can make communication difficult and pose difficult challenges to novices. The field of educational technology, like all worthwhile endeavors, requires thoughtful study, practice, and use. Computers and technology are having an enormous impact on education. As with icebergs, we are only seeing one-tenth of the impact that technology can have on teaching and learning. These many opportunities can be extended through knowledge and understanding of the technology. This chapter offers a glimpse at the fundamentals of computer technology concepts and, hopefully, will whet your appetite for more knowledge.

COMPUTER SYSTEM CONFIGURATIONS

Computer systems contain four interrelated and common components or elements: input, output, processing, and storage. This is the case for large mainframe systems such as those found in business and industry or university computer centers that can serve many users at once, as well as for personal computers. An understanding of these four common building blocks offers an easy way to begin a study of computers. Computer systems consist of hardware and software. Hardware refers to the physical equipment and mechanical-electronic devices used in a system. A home stereo system, for example, may have a receiver, tape player, CD player, and other components that are considered hardware devices. In a similar manner, computers require hardware such as monitors, printers, keyboards, disk drives, CD-ROM drives, and other peripheral devices.

Computer systems also require software, which refers to instructions (computer programs and documentation) and data (information to be processed). To continue the analogy to a home stereo system, software might be compared to records, tapes, CDs, and the manuals that provide instruction for using the stereo system. While hardware may seem the more apparent and important part of the total system, the computer is useless and can perform no operation without instructions in the form of software.

Computers require some type of input device that permits the user to enter data into the system. Input devices may include the familiar typewriter-style keyboard, optical scanning devices, electronic media digitizers, sophisticated sensors, MIDI controller keyboards, cameras, or a microphone for voice input. In a similar manner, output devices provide the user with the finished or processed data, which have been acted on by the computer. Common output hardware includes monitors, printers, and speakers for sound or music.

Processing is at the heart of the computer. This is where data are received and acted on (processed) through a set of instructions. Finally, all computers contain some type of storage device for holding both large amounts of data and the instructions for operating on that data. Each of these four components is discussed later in more detail. Because most readers will relate this information to personal computers or microcomputers such as the IBM-PC or Macintosh, discussions deal primarily with these systems.

INPUT DEVICES

Input devices provide a means for the user to communicate with the computer, or, more specifically, with the central processing unit (CPU). In other words, input devices convert data to a form the computer can understand. The most common input devices are the keyboard and mouse. Most standard keyboards consist of 101 keys and use the alphanumeric layout common to typewriters. The keyboard looks like a typewriter with a few additional keys that perform computer-specific functions. The exact layout of the keyboard may vary slightly from vendor to vendor, but most will have a number of similar features and keys (e.g., ENTER, function keys labeled F1, F2, etc., directional arrow keys, Control [Ctrl], Escape [Esc], and so on). These extra keys allow the user to control software and certain computer functions.

Pointing devices such as a mouse, joystick, trackball, light pen, touch screen, or stylus tablet may be used in conjunction with the keyboard to enter data. These pointing devices allow the user to specify a location or create images on the computer screen and execute a command (point and click).

Data entry has also been greatly enhanced through various types of optical scanning input devices. Scanners digitize printed images, which means that they transform documents and photographs into digital data that the computer can store, edit, and transmit. Optical character recognition (OCR) provides for data entry in several forms: optical mark sensing (such as in the test answer form); bar codes such as those used to enter prices on market products and in multimedia applications; label scanners such as those used on price tags and library materials for circulation; and sheet scanners that eliminate manual entry of pages of text. Multipurpose office machines combine a scanner, printer, copier, fax, and modem into a single unit.

A relatively new input device that has rapidly grown in popularity is the digital camera. With a digital camera, the user eliminates the need to take a photograph, process it, scan it, and enter the picture into the computer system. Most digital cameras look similar to regular point-and-shoot film cameras. They do not, however, use film; instead they record the image on a semiconductor chip. The image is converted into tiny electronic dots, or pixels, that are stored in the camera's memory. The image can be transferred to the computer and saved as a file, edited, and used by word processing, desktop publishing, or graphics programs.

There are numerous other input devices ranging from voice recognition, magnetic ink character recognition (MICR, which is used for bank checks), digitizers that can convert video from analog sources such as camcorders, to keyboard controllers for electronic music composition. In all cases, the purpose of the input devices is the same: to provide data in a digital form that the computer can interpret and process.

OUTPUT DEVICES

Output devices serve the opposite purpose of input devices. They provide a means for the computer to communicate processed data in a form that is intelligible to the user. Common output devices are printers and monitors. Printers produce "hard copy" output or permanent documents (often termed "printouts") such as reports or lists and are available in several types.

The ink-jet printer produces high or letter-quality output and has become increasingly popular as its prices have decreased. Ink-jet printers use a print head that shoots ink at the paper to produce characters and graphics. They can be purchased for less than $200 and can produce near laser-quality print. Color ink-jet printers that produce multicolor output are also becoming popular and inexpensive. Ink-jet printers are an excellent option for home, classroom, or light office work, but are not well suited for heavy work loads. Liabilities of ink-jet printers in high volume applications are the cost of the ink cartridges and overall speed of output.

Another type of printer, the dot-matrix printer, presses tiny pins against a ribbon to print dots on paper. The resulting dots form characters in a manner not unlike the familiar sports scoreboard. Dot-matrix printers are among the least expensive printers and have decreased in popularity. They are somewhat noisy and produce comparatively low-quality documents. Most dot-matrix printers can overlap the dots to produce near-letter-quality appearance; however, if the density of the dots is low and the ribbon happens to be a bit dry, the type can be difficult to read. Dot-matrix printers are useful for printing multiple layer forms and routine documents that do not need to be letter-quality or for student use in the classroom or computer laboratory.

Laser printers use a technology similar to laser photocopiers and can efficiently produce high quality (near-typeset-quality) output. Because they are also quiet and require little maintenance, they have become part of a standard office system. Laser printers produce a full page at a time using office photocopier technology (a laser beam creates an image on a light-sensitive drum). This image is transferred to regular paper by fusing toner to the page at a high temperature. Laser printers have become more affordable in recent years (starting at around $400). More expensive laser printers provide faster output, better print quality, have graphics capabilities, and withstand heavier workloads. Inexpensive laser printers generally produce 4 pages per minute while heavy-duty printers designed for offices can produce 24 pages per minute.

Monitors (also referred to as video display terminals or VDTs, terminals, or screens) display information on television-type or CRT (cathode ray tube) devices. The monitor is one of the most important devices in the system. A sharp and focused display can be a valuable asset to the user, while a fuzzy image will result in eyestrain and general discomfort. Monitors may display only one color (monochrome monitors) or multiple colors (16, 256, or millions of colors). They may also have varying resolutions, that is, the capability to produce finer and smoother images, according to the size and number of pixels (dots). The more pixels (the dots of light on the screen) displayed, the higher the quality and the sharper the image. High quality monitors are, of course, more expensive and will have a low dot pitch (the space between pixels), such as .28 or .25, and are noninterlaced (reducing flicker in the display). Monitors, like televisions, come in different sizes, generally in 14-, 15-, 17-, and 20-inch sizes (measured diagonally from one corner of the screen to the other), as well as large screens for room-size presentations.

PROCESSING

The system unit of the microcomputer contains the central processing unit (CPU) as well as the computer's memory and other components that make the system function. The CPU is the "brains" of the computer; it handles all calculations and executes the prescribed commands and processing that are required. The power of modern CPUs is awesome as regards speed, instruction sets, and capability to address memory. The type of CPU used in the computer determines the speed or processing power of the system. For example, the original IBM PCs of the early 1980s used 8086, 8088, and (later) 80286 CPUs. More recent PC systems use Intel Pentium processors or similar CPUs. The speed of a CPU is measured in megahertz (MHz). This number represents how fast it can process data. For example, a Pentium II/266 operates at 266 MHz. The Apple Macintosh computer (and clones) uses versions of the PowerPC chip.

The PowerPC Alliance—Apple, Motorola, and IBM—joined to produce a PowerPC microprocessor that provides speeds that surpass speeds of computers with higher MHz ratings. The 233 or 266 MHz PowerPC G3 was built specifically for the Mac OS (operating system).

DATA STORAGE

The computer's memory stores data and instructions during the processing cycle. All of us are familiar with data storage in some form. We keep information (store data) in checkbook registers about deposits and checks written. The teacher's gradebook is a data storage device. From time to time, these data are retrieved as we balance bank accounts or prepare students' grades for report cards. Computers primarily use two different types of storage: primary memory, which includes RAM (random access memory) and ROM (read-only memory), and secondary storage (e.g., disk, tape, CD-ROM). Because memory is an important topic, each type is briefly discussed.

PRIMARY MEMORY

Random access memory (RAM, main memory, or primary storage) is the temporary residence for the operating system, data, and instructions during the data processing cycle or work session. Data can be accessed at very high speeds—near the speed of light—from RAM. RAM, however, is volatile, which means that when the power is turned off, the contents are deleted and lost. Random access memory is measured in megabytes (MB) or millions of bytes where a byte represents the unit of measure of computer storage (a byte is roughly equivalent to one character of information or one keystroke). Because of the sophistication of today's software, it is not uncommon for even the most basic personal computers to have 32 to 64 MB of RAM. RAM chips can be of several different types (DRAM, EDO, or SRAM); these memory types have different operating or access time speeds. Generally speaking, the more RAM the system has, the more efficiently it will operate.

Read-only memory (ROM) is a special type of primary storage where data and instructions are permanently stored. ROM chips commonly store instructions required by the computer during the start-up ("system booting") process. ROM is also used in peripheral devices such as printers and modems. ROM is nonvolatile and the contents are not lost when power is turned off. Like RAM, data can be accessed at very high speeds, but memory contents cannot be altered.

SECONDARY STORAGE

Secondary or auxiliary storage is principally used to store data or instructions until they are required in a work session. Technically, secondary storage devices also qualify as input/output devices because they read data and instructions (input) and store processed data (output). Common forms of secondary storage are magnetic disks (hard drives, diskettes and floppy disks), magnetic tapes, and CD-ROMs. Magnetic disks are the most frequently used medium in microcomputer systems and provide large amounts of reusable storage. Removable disks (diskettes) are available in 5.25-inch and 3.5-inch types (although the 5.25-inch types are rarely used today); typically, diskettes will store well over a megabyte. How disks store data is not important to our discussion, but it is important to have an understanding of the critical role secondary storage plays in the information processing cycle.

Hard or fixed disk drives store the computer's operating system and the user's software programs and data. They operate much like diskettes but are not removable and have a much greater storage capacity. Hard drive storage is usually measured in gigabytes (a gigabyte is a billion bytes or characters). They operate much faster than removable disks and are more convenient.

Magnetic tape storage systems are among the oldest form of mass data storage on large mainframe computers. Magnetic tape systems for personal computers are gaining popularity as convenient devices for file backup and archiving. The contents of an entire hard drive can be written to a magnetic tape only slightly larger than an audiocassette tape. Such systems for data backup are useful in almost any computing environment.

Optical data storage media such as the CD-ROM (Compact Disc–Read Only Memory) have gained popularity in recent years. CD-ROM discs look identical to the popular compact disk (CD) music medium and use the same technology. A typical CD-ROM can store over 600 megabytes of data including text, sounds, music, and images. They are especially useful for encyclopedias, dictionaries, databases, directories, games, and multimedia applications. A new generation of disks called DVD-ROM is starting to appear. These can store approximately 5 gigabytes of data. Later models will store much more.

COMPUTER COMMUNICATIONS

Recently, communication between and among computers has become one of the more frequently discussed topics in the area of educational technology. In fact, networks in schools and school districts are becoming quite commonplace. Computer communication simply means sending and receiving computer or digital data and may be through telecommunication or through a computer network.

TELECOMMUNICATIONS

Telecommunications is one of the rapidly growing applications of computers in all fields including education. Enormous amounts of information are accessible through online databases, bulletin boards, and electronic mail systems. Systems such as America On-Line (AOL), CompuServe, and the Internet offer an amazing and interesting array of educational potentials. There are also over 10,000 public electronic bulletin boards. Thousands of databases are available through online services, and newspapers, actual newswire sources, stock quotes, weather reports, legislation reports, and banking services, as well as games and entertainment are accessible through telecommunications.

To initiate telecommunications applications, specific hardware and software are required. In addition to standard personal computer hardware, a modem or network is needed. Communications software commands the modem and provides the capabily to receive and handle information.

Essentially, a modem is a device that allows digital data produced by computers to be transmitted over commercial telephone lines. This is accomplished by converting digital signals (zeros and ones) to audio signals (analog data) that are relayed much like a regular conversation. Modem speeds are measured in bits per second (bps) and are typically in the range of 28,800 (28K) bps to 56,000 (56K) bps. The faster the modem speed, the faster files can be transferred with high-speed transfer. Newer modems can also send and receive faxes as well as data.

Telecommunications has become one of the most frequently referenced applications of personal computers along with the more familiar uses such as word processing, database systems, spreadsheets, and graphics. Educational applications of telecommunications are virtually limitless.

NETWORKS

A computer does not have to operate as an independent, isolated machine. Computers can share files and peripheral devices. This system is called "networking," and can be as simple as two computers sharing files or sharing software. Networks can also be complex, involving thousands of computers sharing software, databases, printers, and other devices.

The computer uses a networking port and network software to accomplish this operation. Ports allow data to be transferred from the computer to the networking cable and through the system to the proper device. All Macintoshes come with networking ports, but only certain newer models of IBM-compatible systems include these ports. If not present in the computer, network interface cards can be added. The cards fit inside the computer in one of the internal expansion slots.

Generally, networks are classified as Local Area Networks (LANs) or Wide Area Networks (WANs). A LAN is basically two or more standalone computers that are directly connected in some small, well-defined space (e.g., a room, building, or campus). Typically, computers in a LAN share certain peripheral devices such as modems, printers, or hard disk drives as well as programs and information. This ability to share hardware and software is an important advantage of LANs. For example, several computers may access a quality laser printer or color plotter. Networks also allow users to communicate via electronic mail (e-mail). Site licenses for popular software to be used at multiple stations can offer significant cost savings to institutions. In addition, users can share the same data sets (updating them as well as retrieving them) and can utilize instructional packages on the LAN.

Computers and other devices in a LAN are connected with special cables (e.g., coaxial cable) using special network software and cards installed in each system. The respective computers are called "nodes" and the configuration is termed the network's "topology." Network topologies carry names like star, ring, bus, or tree networks. Programs that control the network are called "network operating systems."

Retrofit of facilities to accommodate computer networks, especially in school buildings more than a few years old, is a subject of special interest. As mentioned before, considerable cost savings as well as efficiency of use can be achieved through use of networks. Also, communications in the building can provide electronic mail capabilities as well as general data transfer (e.g., attendance reports and student grades).

COMPUTER SOFTWARE

Even a brief discussion and overview of computers and computing is incomplete without consideration of software. Software refers to computer programs, procedures and routines used in a data processing system. Usually, software or computer programs refer specifically to processing instructions written in a language or format intelligible to the computer. Software is generally categorized as systems software, or operating systems software, and applications software. System software directs the functions and operation of the total computer system. The most common type of system software is the disk operating system. Applications software, as the name suggests, includes programs that are associated with particular user tasks, needs, or activities such as word processing, spreadsheets, or filing systems. A third category of software consists of computer programming languages that permit computer instructions to be provided in a form that is more intelligible to the user.

OPERATING SYSTEMS

Concepts of operating systems can lead to a lengthy and complex discussion, in part, because of the importance of this topic. Therefore, we only discuss a few fundamental points and assume that additional reading will follow. An operating system is a program or software that controls the overall operation of the computer. This "low-level" but essential software schedules tasks, allocates storage, handles the interface to peripheral devices, and provides a user interface when no application program is running. It is the master control program responsible for system start-up or system "booting" as well as interaction with peripheral devices (monitors, printers, storage devices, etc.). It also defines how memory is controlled, where data are stored, how files are handled, and how user interfaces are managed.

Different computers and manufacturers may use vastly different operating systems, making compatibility among computers difficult or impossible. Common operating systems for microcomputers are MS-DOS (Microsoft Disk Operating System), CP/M, UNIX, OS/2, Apple's PRODOS, the Apple Macintosh OS operating system, and Microsoft Windows.

APPLICATION SOFTWARE

The microcomputer industry would not exist to the extent it does if it were not for the application software industry. This category of software addresses specific needs of the user.

It is difficult to classify applications software, but one distinct and important area has been termed "productivity software." This refers to software that enhances the user's effectiveness and ability to accomplish certain tasks with greater speed, efficiency, and accuracy. Types of application software include word processing, spreadsheets, filing or database management systems, desktop publishing, communications/fax, presentation managers, graphics systems, and personal finance systems.

Another area of application software includes educational software—programs designed specifically to provide and/or manage instruction. Typically, such software has programs included for drill and practice, tutorials, inquiry, and problem solving. Only in the past few years have private, independent vendors made an aggressive entry into this market. The growth of educational acquisitions of computers, fueled by decreasing hardware costs and increasing public interest, has begun to make the field of educational software a profitable market for private enterprise. Of course, there exist many specialized types of applications tailored for well-defined requirements. Examples include statistical packages, computer-assisted design (CAD) and manufacturing software, profession-specific programs (e.g., legal, medical, architectural, and scientific), and many others.

PROGRAMMING LANGUAGES

Programming languages allow one to interact with the computer for the purpose of providing instructions. Any computer—mainframe or personal computer—requires instructions to perform even the most trivial task. Instructions are provided in the form of the computer program. Just as humans use languages such as English, Spanish, Japanese, and so forth to communicate, so do users employ computer languages to communicate with a computer. There are literally hundreds of computer languages that are classified in areas such as machine languages, assembly languages, and high-level languages. There are also application-specific languages associated with such uses as database management and educational software development (often these programs are termed authoring languages).

High-level programming languages carry rather strange names because they are often acronyms. A few of the more common high-level programming languages are:

- BASIC (**B**eginner's **A**ll-Purpose **S**ymbolic Instructional **C**ode) is a commonly used program on microcomputers. It was developed in the 1960s to offer students an easy-to-learn language.

- FORTRAN (**FOR**mula **TRAN**slator) is an older, but still widely used, language that dates to the 1950s. It is designed for scientific and mathematical applications.

- COBOL (**CO**mmon **B**usiness **O**riented **L**anguage) is a language that was developed in the 1950s for, as the name suggests, business and industry applications.

- Pascal (named for the French mathematician) is a popular instructional language that is well suited for teaching structured programming.

- C is a powerful, yet concise, language widely used in the development of applications software.

- Ada (named after Lady Ada Lovelace, daughter of Lord Byron, and perhaps the first computer programmer) is a powerful language developed primarily for Department of Defense applications.

- Java is a new programming language that is being developed by Sun Microsystems. Java makes it possible to incoporate small applications and computer code on a Web page. When the Web page is accessed, the Java code is sent along with the HTML (Hypertext Markup Language) code.

The commercial availability of a wide range of applications software packages has greatly reduced or, in many cases, eliminated the need for programming knowledge in order to be a productive computer user.

SUMMARY

Powerful computer systems and associated technology are now affordable in schools for both instructional and administrative applications. What began as a novelty for some in the mid-1970s with the introduction of the early microcomputers such as the TRS-80, Apple II, and Commodore has become an essential instructional tool. Selection of the "right" system for a school continues to be a perplexing task for many educators and decision-makers. This is not likely to change, as the power and complexity of the technology continues to evolve. Choices between platforms (MS-DOS or Windows or Macintosh), levels of computing power, and costs can lead to difficult decisions.

There are no absolute rules. In general, educational institutions, like businesses, should not be tempted to purchase "yesterday's technology" even though the price may be tempting. The cost of upgrades and replacements may be even more expensive. In other words, invest in the future and tomorrow's applications.

3

INSTRUCTIONAL COMPUTER APPLICATIONS

Computer-Assisted Instruction (CAI)

The roots of computer-assisted instruction (CAI) can be traced back many years, even into the 1960s. Although it is beyond the scope and purpose of this overview of CAI, the reader is encouraged to peruse some of the seminal works accomplished during these formative years as they can be instructive to future applications. It also should be noted that the terms computer-assisted instruction (CAI), computer-based instruction (CBI), and computer-based education (CBE) are often used interchangeably. In all of these systems, the computer is generally accepted to be a principal source of instruction (as opposed to an object of instruction as in computer science). Most instructional or CAI software has been classified into several types according to the function it serves: drill and practice software, tutorial software, simulation software, and problem-solving software.

Drill and Practice Software

Drill and practice software provides opportunities for students to practice what they have learned from other sources (such as the teacher), with the computer providing immediate feedback about their results. Sometimes drill and practice software is viewed as little more than an electronic ditto sheet or workbook page, but research has shown that the opportunity for varied practice and the knowledge of correct results are critical to mastering basic skills. Students are usually more excited when working at the computer than when completing a workbook page. They will generally work longer at the computer and good drill and practice programs will not allow them to make the same mistakes over and over again. The software program will offer corrections and hints for improvement to the students. Some drill and practice programs allow students to interact with problems in a stimulating, game-like setting; many students find this highly motivating. Many of the earlier drill and practice applications concentrated on basic skills (e.g., spelling and math facts) but these applications have evolved and improved with the technology.

TUTORIAL SOFTWARE

When the computer actually presents new information and provides instruction as well as the opportunity to practice and to test understanding, the software is classified as tutorial software. Tutorial software can assist and encourage students to progress at their own pace. Frequently, tutorial software requires a student's input to proceed to a higher level of instruction. Interactive tutorial programs can provide students with individualized instruction and repetition that may lead to enhanced student performance. Tutorials generally provide the sequencing, structure, and consistency important in instruction for many students. Tutorial programs range from simple to extremely complex in design. Many are linear, with all students completing the same program, although the pace may be different for each student. Complex programs may offer multiple branching opportunities, with different responses taking the student to different parts of the program for review, remediation, or advanced information. With extremely complex tutorial programs, it is possible that two students may go through the program on completely different paths as well as at a different pace. However, learning outcomes for the program are the same.

SIMULATION SOFTWARE

Simulations offer students an opportunity to see the consequences of their choices and often employ graphic demonstrations of abstract concepts. Simulations model reality and real-life situations, but also allow students to interact with the experience without the risks or expenses that might otherwise be involved. Students involved in simulations may be asked to use math skills, to develop problem-solving strategies, and to use observation and note-taking skills. Simulations usually involve reading skills, mathematical skills, and reasoning skills. Much has been written about the need for students to acquire problem solving and higher order thinking skills. Simulation software has the capacity to address that need.

Problem-Solving Software

Problem-solving software allows students to develop higher-order thinking skills through interaction with the computer and associated technology. Software of this type generally introduces students to one or more approaches to problem solving and gives practice in identification of the problem, finding alternative solutions, selecting appropriate strategies, and evaluating the results of decisions made. Problem-solving software provides excellent opportunities for cooperative learning when pairs or teams of students work together with the software. Problem-solving software is available for all levels.

Computer-Managed Instruction (CMI)

Computer-managed instruction (CMI) refers to the use of a computer system to manage information about learner performance and learning resource options in order to prescribe and control individualized lessons. While early systems merely tracked a student's progress on a particular piece of software and reported it to the teacher on request, today's sophisticated systems can diagnose learning problems, remediate the learner in those specific areas, monitor, and report the student's progress. Systems can even automatically adjust to the student's ability, learning style, and interests. Today's modern CMI systems, known as integrated learning systems (ILS), offer large systems of individualized instruction in one or more subject areas managed by the computer. These are generally offered through a network of computers that are connected to a central "file server," which stores the instructional programs and keeps track of student progress. This type of CMI offers seamless curricula and emphasizes basic skills for many students as a part of their overall instructional programs.

COMPUTER-ENHANCED INSTRUCTION (CEI)

Computer-enhanced instruction (CEI) refers to using computers to bring additional dimensions to traditional teaching methods that may be impractical without the aid of a computer. This includes using the computer to create instructional materials, slide shows and videotapes, worksheets, tests, visuals, bulletin board materials, rewards, incentives, games, and displays. CEI also includes using the computer to increase personal productivity for teachers through gradebook programs and word processing programs.

Teachers who use computers in these ways find that instruction is indeed enhanced. They are not only more productive, but are more organized because of better record keeping and because of the thought and planning required to produce effective, computer-generated instructional materials. The learning environment is more appealing when materials are neatly and professionally generated.

COMPUTER AS AN INSTRUCTIONAL TOOL
(APPLICATION SOFTWARE)

The computer can also be used as a tool in the teaching and learning process by both students and teachers.

WORD PROCESSING PROGRAMS

Word processing programs can be used by students to write papers, reports, letters, and stories. Documents can be filed, edited, printed, and published for others to read. Built-in spelling and grammar checkers assist those who sometimes have difficulty improving their written communications. Frequently, word processing programs offer the ability to make the written word look better through many styles and sizes of available fonts, through color, and through a wide variety of formatting choices. Much has been written about the positive effects of word processing programs in improving writing skills and in changing the way students process information.

DATABASE PROGRAMS

Database programs assist in the organization and retrieval of information. Using database programs helps students think about the world systematically. As the number of databases available to students increases, this technology can help them access information needed for research, presentations, and decision making. Database programs require students to break large amounts of material into small chunks and to compare data in a systematic way. Information management is becoming an essential life skill; databases are programs that allow people to manage information. Learning to use databases gives students more control over their own learning, as well as access to information. With a database program, students can use the computer to put things in alphabetical, numerical, or sequential order. Students can compare and contrast data, test hypotheses, and organize and share information.

SPREADSHEET PROGRAMS

Spreadsheet programs assist students in computational skills, analyzing data, and predicting outcomes. They help students with mathematics in much the same ways as word processing programs assist composition. Spreadsheet programs organize numerical information into rows and columns and are useful in gathering, calculating, and analyzing numerical data. These programs generally contain presentation graphs and database capabilities as well.

GRAPHICS PROGRAMS

Graphics programs help students communicate information, increase visual literacy, and make abstract concepts and ideas easier to understand. Graphics programs allow the nonartist to create diagrams, drawings, and illustrations without a great deal of talent. They make it easy to draw circles and straight lines, to provide vibrant colors and patterns, and to add interesting textures and shading. They can also encourage discovery learning and promote general problem-solving strategies.

TELECOMMUNICATIONS PROGRAMS

Telecommunications programs allow students to share information they have created and to access information from other students and other sources. Using a telecommunication program and a modem, students can send electronic mail (e-mail) and access a wide variety of electronic bulletin boards and databases. The computer can be used to contact people and to locate resources outside of the classroom and school.

INTEGRATED PROGRAMS

Integrated programs not only provide all of these capabilities, but also allow the student to combine the information created in different parts of the program. For example, the student can write a letter using a word processing program, include a chart created in the graphics portion of the spreadsheet, and address and mail it to a number of selected people using the database. Tool or application software can be used across the curriculum and in the workplace.

LOGO

LOGO is a computer language that has been used by students for discovery learning. Using LOGO, students enter a simple command in English to make a "turtle" move on the screen. For example, students can type FORWARD 10 and see the turtle move ahead, drawing a line 10 units long. If they want the line longer, they experiment with the FORWARD command, substituting larger numbers, until it draws a line of the length they want. Simple commands move the turtle, change the color of the line, turn the turtle, and repeat the commands any number of times. Students experiment with commands, observe the movement of the turtle, and design more complex sets of commands that they name as procedures. The procedures can become more and more complex as students create problems and discover ways to solve them.

LOGO reinforces many basic skills. Command words in LOGO must be spelled correctly for the computer to recognize them. They can be edited, reinforcing skills in language arts. Students also learn about shapes, angles, patterns, repetition, estimation, averaging, and many other mathematical concepts while using LOGO. LOGO can also be used with LEGO blocks to learn scientific principles and to automate tasks.

AUTHORING PROGRAMS

Without knowing complex computer languages, such as those mentioned in Chapter 2, students and teachers can create their own computer programs using authoring programs. Several inexpensive programs—HyperCard, Linkway, HyperStudio, and TutorTech—were among the first to allow both teachers and students to create their own programs by using simple menus and a "point-and-click" interface.

Many teachers use authoring programs to create their own instructional software. While this can take a great deal of the teacher's time, it can also assist the teacher in the organization of lesson content and in its presentation. Additionally, software can be tailored to the teacher's style, the students' individual needs, or both.

Students use these same authoring programs to create instructional software for other students in their class or other classes, to prepare multimedia reports, to demonstrate their creativity, and to demonstrate their own learning. Because students generally have more time, and often have more computer experience than adults, it is not unusual to see student-generated programs which show a great deal more sophistication than those of their teachers.

While all of these programs are still in use in many schools, newer programs with enhancements and additional features can now be used, including Digital Chisel, HyperStudio, Linkway Live, Multimedia Scrapbook, and ToolBook. These programs can easily access peripheral devices such as

CD audio, CD-ROM, photo-CD, videodisc, and videotape to create multimedia presentations or programs.

PRESENTATION SOFTWARE

While authoring programs can be used to create presentations, several software programs have been developed especially for this purpose. The improved power and quality, lower cost, and increased accessibility of both computers and liquid crystal display (LCD) panels and other large screen projection devices, make this software almost as popular in education as it is in business. Like authoring programs, presentation software is easy to use. Programs such as Microsoft PowerPoint allow the user to enter information in outline form and then quickly transform the outline to colorful slides with little more than a click of the mouse. Once the content is created, typefaces and colors used in the presentation can easily be changed, transitions between slides can be added, and special effects on each slide are easily achieved. Moreover, clip art, charts, and digitized sound, music, and movie clips are easy to add to most presentation software. Presentation software also provides a place for the teacher or student to type in important notes and then print them for use during the presentation or as a handout to accompany the presentation.

MULTIMEDIA

The definition of multimedia has changed over time with technology. Once, the term brought to mind slide/tape programs or kits, which included tapes and filmstrips. Today, multimedia centers on computer technology and uses the computer's capability to deliver sound, graphics, full-motion video, and text. Additionally, today's computer-based multimedia can access data and images stored on peripheral devices such as CD-ROMs, videotapes, videodiscs, and the Internet. Multimedia programs are available commercially and can also be created by students using authoring languages mentioned previously.

VIDEODISCS

Interactive videodiscs are another computer-related technology. Videodiscs are similar to videotapes except that information does not have to be accessed in a linear fashion (forward, fast forward, and rewind), but can be accessed randomly, much as the songs on a record or compact disc can be accessed. A videodisc can store full-motion video, text, or thousands of still-frame graphics or slides. It can also contain any combination of these elements. Two audio tracks are available on videodiscs. One track can be used for English and a second track for a foreign language version of the narration. Similarly, one track can be used for a simple narration and the other for a more complex one, or one track can be used for teachers and the other for students.

Interactive videodiscs combine the power of the microcomputer and computer-assisted instruction with the rich images of video. A student using an interactive video program might use the computer to access slides of lions, mollusks, or conifers on a biology disk. Interactive videodiscs allow students to see real-life simulations on the video monitor, and to have their comprehension checked by a computer program. Those who master the competencies can continue to move through the program, while those who need remediation might be looped through a different sequence of instruction about the topic.

Interactive videodiscs can be used to explore a world of audiovisual information from the desktop. Teachers can use the interactive videodisc to prepare a class presentation or to plan individual learning experiences for different students.

CD-ROM

A distant relative of the videodisc is the CD-ROM (compact disc–read only memory). Actually, the CD-ROM is more closely related to the audio compact discs that have almost completely replaced the vinyl phonograph record. A CD-ROM is the same size as an audio CD. Both are read by laser beams using a special CD player. However, the CD-ROM contains digital computer information rather than music.

The primary advantage of CD-ROM is its huge storage capacity. A single CD-ROM can hold approximately 300,000 pages of text or over 1,500 floppy disks worth of information. An entire encyclopedia—every word, article, picture, graph, and table and its index—can be placed on one CD-ROM disc with plenty of spare room. CD-ROMs originally were used for reference materials such as encyclopedias, dictionaries, indexes, and other materials that do not change very often. They are now used for all kinds of computer data, but especially for multimedia, which requires a large amount of storage space for sound and digital video.

MIDI

MIDI is one of the true breakthroughs in music, electronics, and digital systems. MIDI is an acronym for Musical Instrument Digital Interface. It provides standardization for compatibility among digital musical instruments from various manufacturers. Stated another way, MIDI communicates musical notes, sounds, or events (pitch, volume, dynamics, vibrato, tempo, etc.) in a common language of digital data.

A comparatively recent technology (introduced in 1983), MIDI has and continues to revolutionize the entire music industry, including entertainment and music education. So powerful is this tool that it has completely changed the ways musicians, producers, engineers, and music educators approach their trade. To understand how MIDI systems work, one must first recall how everyday sounds are produced (voice, noise, music—anything we hear). Essentially, any sound is the product of acoustic vibration, ultimately arriving at our ears. Three components define the sound:

- ♦ Pitch (high or low depending on the frequency). Pitch is measured in Hertz (Hz) or cycles per second; most humans have a hearing range from about 20 to 20,000 Hz. Concert A is 440 Hz.

- ♦ Amplitude (volume or loudness). Striking a piano key with a hard attack will produce a louder (higher amplitude) than a soft attack.

♦ Timbre (the color or distinctive characteristic of a sound). Timbre is the component of sound that makes a piano note sound completely different from the same note played on a violin or saxophone.

All of these attributes, as well as the dynamics of how a note is played, must be digitally encoded and communicated among MIDI system components to produce authentic sounds.

Until the late 1960s, instruments relied on either their physical construction (woods, brass, strings, etc.) or analog electric sounds (electronic organs, electric guitars and basses, etc.). Early digital instruments such as the Yamaha DX7 radically changed the way we think about music production. Modern digital music instruments can produce an amazing reproduction of a traditional instrument such as a piano through a technique called "sampling."

Consider a typical MIDI implementation. A musician presses a key on a keyboard (sometimes called a controller or controller keyboard). This action is transmitted to a sound generator or sound module (a synthesizer without a keyboard) where a note is generated or simulated. This sound or signal is then sent to an amplifier and speakers.

This interface between the controller keyboard and the sound module is a critical area for the use of MIDI. A digital code that conveys the way the musician played the note must be sent to the sound module. Physically, the MIDI connection consists of a 5-conductor cable and 5-pin connectors. Conductors 4 and 5 carry a MIDI signal (0 or +5 volts); conductor 2 is a ground wire (conductors 1 and 3 are not used). Theoretically, there is no limit to the number of sound modules a musician might control using this technology.

One of the powerful aspects of MIDI technology is "sequencing." Sequencing is much like using a conventional tape recorder, except that sounds are recorded in tracks digitally rather than in an analog fashion. Sequencers are in many respects like word processors in that music information can be edited on screen, copied, and cut/pasted. When a composition has been recorded and edited to the musician's satisfaction, it can be played through the MIDI system. Popular sequencer programs include Cakewalk, Cubase, Orchestrator Pro, and PowerTracks.

If a printed score is required or lead sheets with lyrics and chord symbols for the choir or band, notational software can handle that task. Software such as Desktop Sheet Music, QuickScore Elite, MusicTime Deluxe, Finale, and ConcertWare are inexpensive but provide powerful solutions.

An extension of the MIDI concept emerged later and is termed General MIDI (GM). This system provided for a further standardization of MIDI files and compositions. More specifically, various instruments are mapped to be consistent among various manufacturers. A particular "patch," for instance, will always be a piano; another will always be a guitar; and so forth. This level of standardization makes the development and compatibility of MIDI files and musical compositions on synthesizers possible. Users can access vast libraries of MIDI files on the Internet, download them, load sequences into their own MIDI systems, and play the files with little or no editing.

MIDI systems have opened a new world of possibilities for music educators. Autoaccompaniment and instructional software such as Band-in-a-Box, The Pianist, Play Piano, and Jazz Guitarist have almost limitless applications. MIDI systems provide a wealth of opportunity for multimedia development and enhancement. Perhaps most importantly, MIDI has bridged the gulf between the musical arts and computer sciences to produce incredible opportunities for teaching, learning, and personal enjoyment.

THE INTERNET

During the past two decades, few technological innovations have dramatically altered our personal and professional lives to the extent that the Internet has. The particularly exciting part of this phenomenon is that the impact was so unanticipated. It is doubtful that anyone foresaw the extent of the role the Internet would play in the technological revolution. It is even more surprising that it has become a way of life for the average person—just like cable TV, VCRs, and the newspaper! Growth of the Internet is staggering, as is the increase in the number of Internet users. One study, for example, estimates that over 37 million PCs are regularly accessing the Internet in the United States. It is also estimated that there are over 100 million persons online throughout the world!

Where did this intriguing system come from? Did it just materialize overnight? To answer these questions, a brief glance at history can be instructive.

First of all, the Internet is not, technically speaking, a network. It is a network of networks capable of sharing data and information. These networks range in size and complexity from those small systems maintained by an individual to large government, corporate, and university networks. They are able to communicate in a common language thanks to a common network language or protocol called TCP/IP. Here are a few milestones in the Internet's history:

1969, ARPANET: A Department of Defense experiment related to networking defense agencies, contractors, and research universities

1973, FTP: File Transfer Protocol (FTP) is introduced

1980, CSNET: Computer Science NETwork linked computer science departments

1981, BITNET: Network that linked university mainframes

1983, TCP/IP: Introduction of TCP/IP (Transmission Control Protocol/Internet Protocol)

1986, NSFNET: National Science Foundation Network connecting supercomputer centers

1990, ARPANET: ARPANET ceases to exist

1991, Gopher: Gopher (a database communications protocol for locating data files) is released

1991, NSF: NSF lifts restrictions on commercial use of the Internet

1991, Computing Act: High Performance Computing Act, authored by then-Senator Gore, is signed into law

1993, Mosaic: Mosaic (an easy to use Web browser) was developed

1995, Netscape: Netscape goes public (Netscape continues to be the most popular Web browser)

1995, Providers: U.S. Internet traffic now carried by commercial Internet service providers

1996, Browser wars: Netscape and Microsoft fight "browser wars"

1996, Decency Act: Communications Decency Act is passed by Congress

1997, Decency Act: Decency Act ruled unconstitutional

1998, World users: It is estimated that there are over 100 million Internet users online worldwide

The Internet has afforded a boundless resource for teachers in classrooms throughout the world, offering resources that would have been unimaginable a few years ago. Applications are limited only by one's imagination, but here are a few examples:

ELECTRONIC MAIL

E-mail gives teachers an inexpensive but convenient mode of communication both among their colleagues and with students. Students can communicate with other students locally and throughout the world. The collection and sharing of data and information related to classroom activities can introduce new and exciting dimensions to learning. Attachments to files offer a convenient way to exchange pictures, sounds, and other documents.

RESEARCH

The Internet is an enormous reservoir of current information and research materials about almost any topic. This information resource can augment traditional research sources (texts, libraries, etc.) with the most current facts and information. A critical challenge to teachers is helping students discern between "good" information and research materials as compared with information that may not be accurate or valid. The addition of sounds, graphics, and multimedia add to the enrichment possible through this medium.

DISCUSSION GROUPS

Dialogue among Internet users can be a rewarding means of gathering information and insights about topics of study. Discussion groups or newsgroups can allow teachers and students to learn from each other in an efficient manner (without having to arrange face-to-face meetings or playing the dreaded "telephone tag").

FILE TRANSMISSION

Files can be easily transmitted via the Internet. An updated printer driver, new virus protection software, shareware programs, and so on are efficiently sent and retrieved without having to wait days or weeks for conventional delivery.

ONLINE OR LIVE CONFERENCING

Teachers and students can dialogue in real time, have discussions about a current topic, or have a debate. With the necessary audio and video hardware and software, they can see as well as hear.

INTERNET CHALLENGES

Many challenges continue to confront educators as they explore the use of the Internet. The easy access to inappropriate material continues to be a policy issue in most schools. An innocent Internet search may quickly lead to pornography. Free access to the Internet may allow undesirable persons to become part of a discussion group. Educators, however, are dealing with these challenges in creative ways that permit appropriate use of this vast resource without endangering their students. Creativity and knowledge of the medium are central to meeting these challenges.

DISTANCE LEARNING

Student enrollments and population shifts, economic forces, and technological innovations have become powerful catalysts for the development of distance learning systems during the past decade. Once only discussed by institutions of higher education, distance learning is now being considered as a feasible educational delivery option throughout the United States. New waves of technology have led to heavy investments in high-performance telecommunications links to the home and workplace by cable systems, telephone companies, and satellite providers. Paralleling these services has been a completely unforeseen explosion in technological connectivity via the Internet. This worldwide network has created a global village of millions of individuals with an opportunity to receive, create, and exchange information. These same service providers have demonstrated interest in the delivery of educational programs.

A fundamental assumption in distance learning systems is the provision of instruction in a location or time different from that of the instructor. Stated another way, distance learning allows the teaching and learning process to be independent of time and/or place. Typical systems or modes include technology-enhanced classrooms, self-paced learning labs, extended classrooms (classrooms linked to the home or workplace via technology), and classroom-free learning environments. Technologies have included radio, audio conferencing, audio graphics, television, video conferencing, and interactive television.

The culture of educational systems has led to a tension among educational professionals regarding the utility and effectiveness of distance education. As with computer-based education, the expert opinions of educational professionals are mixed. Similarly, distance education is still in its infancy even though examples can be traced back over decades. The educational impact over the past two decades may almost be negligible compared to what we can expect in the near future. Many educators continue to resist and find comfort in traditional models. However, it appears clear that distance education, like educational technology in general, will continue to expand in both K-12 systems and in higher education.

TECHNOLOGY AND SCHOOL RESTRUCTURING

Most informed educators will agree that technology is in their future. They also accept that change has become a key variable in our conceptualization of educational delivery systems. Many educators also believe that the new wave of technology has the power to transform our schools from their century-old industrial model to organizations reflective of an information age. Applications of technology in education do offer promise of meaningful restructuring of United States schools. Technology supports the elusive constructivist view of education that promotes the teacher as facilitator of learning rather than the source of all knowledge. Technology also supports student-centered teaching and learning environments.

Schools that have embraced technological change in instructional delivery have witnessed many dramatic improvements that are consistent with proponents of school restructuring. For example, computer-based education fosters the concept of small-group instruction rather than traditional lecture modes of delivery. Almost all evaluations of classrooms rich in technology report students to be engaged and active learners. Even the early educational technology systems were found to appeal to students who were the most difficult to reach and were characterized as being among the weaker students. Furthermore, modern multimedia technology embraces the many assets of visual and verbal learning—a component of instruction frequently associated with the restructured school. It is still too soon to know the extent to which technology will be a catalyst or instrument for school restructuring. Technology does offer the possibility for major shifts in teaching practices and organizational paradigms. Perhaps most importantly, technology can be the tool by which teachers can become instructional leaders.

4

PROFILES

Academy of Communications and Multimedia Technology

Goals of Technology Program

- To develop and pioneer quality multimedia presentations that will enhance the educational mission of the school
- To prepare students for the demands and opportunities of the information economy while creating a qualified talent pool for building and maintaining computer networks
- To prepare students for the demands and opportunities of the computer graphics industry by providing the opportunity to learn and master the latest industry standard software packages

Keywords

- Graphics
- Multimedia
- Networking

Location

Mainland High School
125 S. Clyde Morris Blvd.
Daytona Beach, FL 32114

Description of School and Community

- Grades 9–12 and 2,000 students
- Approximately 150 teachers
- The area's major industry is tourism and related trades, but the area also supports a growing number of businesses and light industries.

DESCRIPTION OF PROGRAM

Mainland High School offers a school-within-a-school for students interested in multimedia technology, computer networking, computer graphics, television production, journalism, and other technologies being developed and used by business and industry. The Academy of Communications and Multimedia Technology integrates required language arts, social studies, and math courses into academy activities focusing on academic content through project-based technology applications. This academy offers excellent college preparation and an orientation to career opportunities in fields such as advertising, networking, journalism and publishing, multimedia and CD development, and graphic and computer arts.

The learning environment in which students develop their projects is a Macintosh and PC laboratory supplemented with CD-Writers, scanners, printers, digital cameras, networking equipment such as Web servers, switches and routers, and other peripherals. The Cisco Networking Academy facet of the Academy's curriculum is delivered via a micro Web server used with a Web browser. A lab consisting of routers, switches, hubs, workstations, and other Internetworking devices for real-world, hands-on learning situations exists. The television production facet of the program allows students to use a fully equipped television studio that includes two editing facilities and portable filming and editing equipment for on-location work. Multimedia development includes the creation of web documents, quicktime movies using Adobe Premiere, and interactive presentations using programs such as Director and Persuasion.

Business partnerships play an important role in the development of this academy. National business partnerships and their areas of expertise include Adobe Systems for software such as Pagemill, Photoshop, Illustrator, and Pagemaker; Cisco Systems for the Internetworking Academy; Walsworth, Inc. for printing and publishing; Eastman-Kodak Company for digital concepts for systems integration and digital products; Apple Computer for computer design, maintenance, and software development; BellSouth for telecommunications and distance learning; Intel Corporation for network support; Hughes Network Systems for satellite delivery; Gateway 2000 for server and workstations; and IBM for Internet servers. Local partners include Media-Photographics for video productions and photographic services.

Internships with cooperating business partners are offered on a competitive basis. For example, students within the Cisco Networking Academy (a branch of the Academy of Communications and Multimedia Technology) work during summers with the school district's Management and Information Services office to help maintain the school district's wide area network.

SPECIAL OUTCOMES, RESULTS, AND ACCOMPLISHMENTS

- ◆ Quality interactive multimedia presentations have enhanced the educational mission of the school
- ◆ Students have learned to develop and use presentation software in classrooms and meetings.
- ◆ Student technology expertise has been greatly enhanced
- ◆ Students graduating with CCNA certification from Cisco Networking Academy are employable in well-paying computer networking positions. Note: These students are still going to college
- ◆ Students have opportunities to do freelance computer graphics work for local companies and other institutions

DIFFICULTIES (ANTICIPATED AND UNANTICIPATED)

Mainland students constantly have the opportunity to pioneer new developments in technology. There have been some problems with the new software. Students can quickly outpace the capacity of the computers available and Mainland must constantly upgrade equipment to keep the program running due to the rapid advancement of various technologies.

THINGS TO CONSIDER

- ◆ Make sure equipment is upgradeable and has adequate memory and storage.
- ◆ Initial investment in hardware/software is expensive.
- ◆ Try to create a partnership with major companies to help offset costs.
- ◆ When pioneering a new program, be ready for mistakes and learn from them.

COSTS

Hardware: $75,000
Software: $8,000
Staff Development: $6,000
Other: $60,000
                     (contributions from business partners)

CONTACT INFORMATION

Todd White
(904) 226-0300 ext. 0354
e-mail: twhite@mail.volusia.k12.fl.us
Home page: http://www.mainland.volusia.kl2.fl.us

ADVENTURES IN TIME

GOALS OF TECHNOLOGY PROGRAM

- ◆ To have students learn about local history in order to better appreciate their heritage
- ◆ To work with the same information in various types of software so that students better understand how to select the proper software for the desired outcome
- ◆ To encourage students to cooperate with others to produce the pieces of a final product
- ◆ To provide opportunities for computer students and art students to collaborate

KEYWORDS

- ◆ Cooperative learning
- ◆ Desktop publishing
- ◆ Internet
- ◆ Multimedia

LOCATION

Riverton Middle School
121 North 5th West
Riverton, WY 82501

DESCRIPTION OF SCHOOL AND COMMUNITY

- ◆ Grades 6–8
- ◆ Approximately 750 students and 45 teachers
- ◆ The facility is approximately 30 years old and in need of a complete retrofitting for technology
- ◆ Riverton, Wyoming is a small community located near the Wind River Indian Reservation. Since the closure of the uranium mines, the major indus-

tries are tourism and agriculture. A junior college, Central Wyoming College, provides academic opportunities for the community. The population is approximately 85% Caucasian; 10% Native American; and 5% Hispanic.

DESCRIPTION OF PROGRAM

This program is a computer curriculum for a one-semester 7th and 8th grade exploratory class that is designed to expose students to various uses of the computer. Each class of 20 students meets for 45 minutes per day for one semester. Corel Photo-Paint is used for the drawing program, Word 6.0 for word processing, CorelDraw for its text capabilities, Pagemaker 5 for desktop publishing, and PowerPoint for multimedia applications.

The students work through tutorials to learn the software and then complete projects to demonstrate mastery. Students become "travel agents" to an event in the past of Fremont County, Wyoming. Each of the culmination projects support some aspect of this vocation. Students work with the director of the local history museum to generate topics and gather information for the projects. The students are allowed to pick a topic and a group of students with whom to work. Students in the art classes act as illustrators for the project.

The culmination project for Corel Photo-Paint is for the group to work together to design a time machine that has some relevance to their event. The culmination project for Word 6.0 is for each group to collaborate to write an adventure to the event and to write the background information. During this time the art students are completing their pen and ink drawings while other students are using black-and-white hand scanners to digitize them.

The culmination projects for CorelDraw are to develop a title for the project, a logo for the travel agency, and a travel poster. At this point participants also use Snappy to capture a color picture of each student.

For the Pagemaker project, all the pieces are brought together. Each student creates a three-fold travel brochure using the pieces they had created in their groups. The pictures and stories are placed, but each student can decide where to put each picture and how he or she wants to individualize the blurbs that are typed in Pagemaker. The students print black and white edit copies with the HPIII networked printer and then two final color copies on heavier paper with the HP560C printer. They then choose one brochure from each group and replace the individual picture with a group picture. Multiple copies of the final brochures are printed and placed in a brochure stand at the Riverton Museum. See page 57 for an example: The Farlow Wolf Roundup.

Using PowerPoint, each student creates a slide show to sell the adventure. They again use all the pieces created in the various software programs as part of the presentation.

Finally, all the pieces are put together on the Riverton Middle School Web site (http://www.fremont25.k12.wy.us/RMS/project/project.htm).

On the evening of the final day of the semester, the group holds an open house for their families. Students show them their PowerPoint presentations, "Snapp" everyone, and view the Web pages in the Media Center.

SPECIAL OUTCOMES, RESULTS, AND ACCOMPLISHMENTS

The students enjoyed working with the historical information. Writing the adventures was much more interesting than just writing reports. The general level of awareness of local history was greatly enhanced.

The students became proficient at using the various software programs. There was more continued usage of software presented earlier in the semester as they decided to edit a document or graphic again before using it in Pagemaker or PowerPoint.

Students have received e-mail from people all over the country with comments about their Internet Web site. It is being used as a resource for information about the area.

DIFFICULTIES (ANTICIPATED AND UNANTICIPATED)

The problems encountered were mostly hardware related. The computers did not have enough memory to support editing some of the graphics that were scanned.

Students also discovered that their video cards only supported 16 colors. The network became very slow when working with the large PowerPoint presentations. The computers used were 486SX33s with no hard drives.

COSTS

Hardware: The project was completed in an existing computer lab with a Novell network server. This cost would depend on the type of computer network installed.

Software: CorelDraw was purchased after newer versions were available for $100 per computer. Microsoft Office Professional was purchased with a MULP agreement at $35 per computer. Pagemaker was purchased in 5-packs at $550 for five computers.

Peripherals: Logitech hand scanners are now available for under $200. (A good flatbed scanner can now be purchased for a similar price.) The Snappy video capture system is under $200. The HP560C cost $500, but color printers are now much less. The color cartridges cost under $30. They used about 5 to print all the brochures. Newer models have replaced the HPIII and the prices vary.

CONTACT INFORMATION

Bev Fast
Computer Teacher
(307) 856-9443
e-mail: bevfast@trib.com

The Farlow Wolf Roundup

August 13, 1917

Our Time Machine

You will begin your two weeks stay in Lander. We will start by introducing you to the Farlow family. Then they will take you to start the wolf roundup. You will sleep in a wagon, and you will eat cornbread with molasses on it. To drink you will have water and on special occasions you will have cider.

You will get to ride a horse or mule. If you wish you may ride in the wagon. You will get two meals a day, breakfast and supper. When you get to the center of the roundup you will get to watch them shoot a young boy's pet coyote so be prepared.

You will travel through rough terrain, like the Muskrat Creek, Willow Springs, Beaver Creek, Wind River Creek, and Company Creek. You will also have to go over some mountains and some hills.

We hope you will enjoy the pretty scenery and the little animals. We wish that you would stay near the wagon train so that no one will get lost or will get attacked by some vicious animals. If you do wander off or get lost, yell for help and we will be looking for you. If you do decide to come, contact the operator and have her/him contact the Wolf Roundup in Lander, Wyoming.

The Farlow Wolf Roundup started August 13th, 1917. The first gun fire of the organization for the big wolf

APPLE CLASSROOMS OF TOMORROW—TEACHER DEVELOPMENT CENTER

GOALS OF TECHNOLOGY PROGRAM

- To encourage students' initiative, independence, and cooperative learning
- To develop critical thinking skills through work on realistic situations that require students to gather, analyze, and manage information
- To provide an interdisciplinary model of instruction
- To allow students to support each other in their learning and to seek to involve the staff, students, and community
- To study the effects on teaching and learning if teachers and students have total access to a technology-rich environment
- To provide a forum for discussing issues related to technology integration, alternative assessment, and collaborative instruction

KEYWORDS

- Cooperative learning
- Multimedia
- Restructuring
- Staff development

LOCATION

West High School
Columbus Public Schools
179 South Powell Avenue
Columbus, OH 43204

DESCRIPTION OF SCHOOL AND COMMUNITY

- ◆ Grades 9–12
- ◆ Approximately 1350 students
- ◆ Approximately 90 teachers
- ◆ Facility is approximately 69 years old
- ◆ West High School is one of 17 urban high schools in the city of Columbus. Student population offers a diverse heritage with 45% African American, 45% Caucasian, and 10% Asian

DESCRIPTION OF PROGRAM

Using the Macintosh as a tool, randomly chosen students study mathematics, science, English, social studies, and various computer business applications in an interdisciplinary approach through team teaching. The students utilize word processing, database systems, spreadsheets, desktop publishing, desktop video, interactive laser discs, robotics, and Web publishing as they learn the prescribed course of study. Art and music are included as students learn skills in multimedia presentations. Technology is used to enhance the curriculum, not replace it.

The classrooms have a 1:3 ratio of computers to students. Virtually all computers in the school are connected to the Internet on a T1 line along with a file server, Web server, and printers on the same Ethernet network within the building.

Software used in the Apple Classroom of Tomorrow (ACOT) Program includes Pagemaker, ClarisWorks, HyperStudio, PageMill, Netscape, Excel, Microsoft Works, and HyperCard.

SPECIAL OUTCOMES, RESULTS, AND ACCOMPLISHMENTS

- ◆ West High School is a SchoolNet Training Center (Technology Learning Center (TLC)) for central Ohio

- The school is one of three national teacher training centers funded by the National Science Foundation
- Real-world success for students has led to national and international recognition and over 4,000 visitors from 22 countries
- Student competencies include dynamic exploration and representation of information; experimentation and problem solving; social awareness and confidence; effective communication; computer use; independence; expertness and collaboration; and a positive orientation to the future
- Several of Columbus' public schools, as well as other districts, are using this instructional technology model

DIFFICULTIES (ANTICIPATED AND UNANTICIPATED)

In the beginning stages, ACOT teachers had to continually reevaluate their old methods of teaching, while being willing to take risks and try out new ideas in the classroom. Teachers had to allow their students to accept more responsibility for their own education. Teachers adopted the knowledge construction approach in which students create, assemble, and produce their own products, demonstrating understanding and mastery of academic goals.

Additional time is required for teachers to learn new technologies with their students. Also, teachers have to adopt new and different student assessment methods. Evaluation strategies, for example, might be quite different when students present before the class their own multimedia project.

THINGS TO CONSIDER

Some modifications had to be made by Columbus Public Schools for its other high schools:

- Add Macintosh Writing Centers to all schools. These can be used by the entire school (West High School presently has a students to computer ratio of 3:1)

- ◆ Provide productivity stations made up of a Macintosh computer and a LaserWriter printer in all high school journalism departments
- ◆ Add videodisc technology to science departments and social studies departments

COSTS

Hardware: $100,000
                   (Includes: Macintosh systems, printers, videodisc players, CD-ROMs, video boards, LCD panels, cameras, and video decks)
Software: $100,000
Personnel: $60,000
                   (Funded through partnerships with Columbus Public Schools, Apple Computer, and NSF)

CONTACT INFORMATION

Bob Howard
ACOT Coordinator
(614) 365-5952
(614) 365-6970 (Fax)
e-mail: rhoward948@aol.com
http://www.columbus.k12.oh.us/westh/index.html

BioBLAST: A Multimedia Learning Environment to Support Student Inquiry in the Biological Sciences

GOALS OF TECHNOLOGY PROGRAM

- To support an inquiry-based, cooperative-learning approach to teaching biology in accordance with the revised National Science Education Standards
- To design an adventure/exploration scenario within an engaging graphical environment that focuses on the future of space exploration
- To provide a systems-level approach to the study of biological issues that integrates math, science, and technology education within a problem-solving, research-oriented context
- To work with a select cadre of teachers from schools throughout the United States to investigate how an interactive adventure can integrate computer-based resources, tools, and simulations, as well as hands-on labs, to enhance student learning
- To demonstrate how NASA's Advanced Life Support research and data can be adapted to provide valuable and motivating resources that enrich student learning and performance in science, math, and technology education

KEYWORDS

- Biology
- Multimedia

- ◆ QuickTime Virtual Reality (QTVR)
- ◆ Simulation
- ◆ Science
- ◆ Scientific inquiry

LOCATION

NASA Classroom of the Future (COTF)
Center for Educational Technologies
Wheeling Jesuit University
316 Washington Avenue
Wheeling, WV 26003
http://www.cotf.edu

DESCRIPTION OF SCHOOL AND COMMUNITY

The NASA Classroom of the Future (COTF) at Wheeling Jesuit University in Wheeling, West Virginia was funded by the National Aeronautics and Space Administration (NASA) in August 1995 to develop BioBLAST. In addition to the software development group at the COTF, 20 biology teachers from throughout the United States and many scientists affiliated with NASA's Advanced Life Support research program have contributed to the design and development of this product. A final round of classroom testing of BioBLAST began in January 1998.

The COTF was established in 1993 to serve as a research and development facility for innovative applications of educational technologies designed to improve K-14 mathematics, science, and technology education. The COTF mission is to demonstrate how NASA science and engineering research and resources can be combined with advanced educational technologies to create exemplary education curriculum supplements. The COTF is one program within the Center for Educational Technologies (CET) on the Wheeling Jesuit University campus. The CET features video production and broadcasting capabilities as well as educational technologies, computer, and distance-learning facilities, from which pre-service and in-service education programs can be disseminated to schools and teachers nationwide.

DESCRIPTION OF PROGRAM

BioBLAST is a multimedia curriculum supplement for high school biology classes that incorporates NASA's Advanced Life Support (ALS) research. Students learn about basic and applied life sciences research underway at NASA centers and apply their prior knowledge of biological processes during the course of this program. Students use simulation models built by the COTF based on NASA ALS data to develop and test their own designs for a bioregenerative system to support human life outside the safety of Earth's atmosphere. The interactive adventure/simulation framework includes computer-based tools and resources, telecommunications events, and hands-on experiments.

Using NASA's research on Bioregenerative Life Support Systems (BLiSS) provides a systems approach to the study of key biological principles that helps students integrate many of the segmented concepts they learn in biology, math, chemistry, and physics. In designing a biologically-based, regenerative system to support humans in space, students develop a greater understanding of the interdependence of living systems. In addition, BioBLAST brings futuristic scenarios into the classroom, where today's students may be tomorrow's explorers. For example, NASA anticipates having a fully self-sufficient air, water, and food recycling system to support a three-year mission to Mars by the year 2008. This means that students from the age of 15 and up are potential candidates for the projected 2008 international space mission to Mars.

BioBLAST includes these features:

A virtual-reality interface. BioBLAST uses a Quick-Time VR graphical interface in which interactive objects, or "hotspots," are embedded. (See top figure on page 65.) The software is designed to draw students into a futuristic, problem-solving scenario in which teams of students are sent to a lunar research facility. (See bottom figure on page 65.)The facility's tools and resources are used to prepare students for their ultimate goal, to design and test a model for a bioregenerative life-support system (BLiSS) that can support a crew of six for three years.

Main Interface for BioBLAST's simulator
© Wheeling Jesuit University/Classroom of the Future

View of QTVR setting for graphical access to Bio BLAST
tools and resources
© Wheeling Jesuit University/Classroom of the Future

An arcade-style game. On their way to the moon, students are introduced to concepts used in the study of closed life-support systems via an animated adventure game. To save the mythical inhabitants of an imaginary world, students must discover the secrets of their ecosystem.

Laboratory investigations. A set of hands-on, laboratory-based activities focuses on key components of plant production, human requirements, and resource recycling processes. An understanding of these processes helps prepare students to design their own fully functional BLiSS.

Crop parameter input screen from the BioBLAST Plant
Production Simulator
© Wheeling Jesuit University/Classroom of the Future

Computer simulations. Simulation software is included to supplement laboratory activities and to enable students to perform investigations not possible in a typical high school biology lab. Three simulations focus on the three topics covered in the laboratory, and a modeling simulation called BaBS (Build a BLiSS System) is used for the design and testing of each student's own BLiSS. These simulations utilize and give high school students access to current NASA basic and applied research data within the context of NASA's Advanced Life Support research program. They also demonstrate to students the use of computational models in the life sciences, and can stimulate student interest in further investigations in this area.

Computer-based resources. In support of student research, the BioBLAST virtual environment contains over 300 documents, 150 images, and over 40 minutes of video. Documents include a variety of articles from scientific journals, popular magazines, and content written for BioBLAST by life-science subject-matter experts. Video segments include a virtual "mentor" who provides suggestions relevant to students' research activities, as well as interviews with NASA scientists currently involved in advanced life-support research.

Telecommunications. BioBLAST software beta-testing activities, scheduled for the spring of 1998, will include a prototype version of the "Ask a NASA Expert" system. This Web-based resource includes an automated question-and-answer system, together with a "frequently asked questions" database so that experts are not overwhelmed with repeat questions. The support provided by the automated question answering system is designed to test the possibility of handling thousands of BioBLAST student questions being asked on a daily basis. The software is designed to dynamically link student questions with similar questions asked and answered before so that NASA scientists and engineers involved in advanced life-support research are only contacted when new questions are submitted.

Adherence to national education standards. The software is closely linked to the National Research Council Guidelines for Science Education. The student investigations and laboratory experiments built into the sequence of BioBLAST activities address specific topics articulated within the national guidelines for biology, math, and technology education. Student research projects address the goals for promoting student abilities and understanding of the methods of scientific inquiry.

SPECIAL OUTCOMES, RESULTS, AND ACCOMPLISHMENTS

Teacher involvement in development. The teachers participating in the formative evaluation of the BioBLAST software and related materials have shown that there are many viable alternative ways of using the program. The teacher-leaders participating in an extended design team have provided examples from their classroom applications of BioBLAST that show how it can be successfully used with gifted and talented, introductory biology, advanced biology, advanced technology, general biology, and student research elective classes.

Teacher interest and commitment. Teachers who have participated in the formative evaluation activities have been extremely enthusiastic and supportive of this program. This quote from one teacher provides an example of the kind of commitment and support teachers have provided to this project: "I get really excited about BioBLAST. It's an innovative program that allows my students to reach a higher level of thinking. I feel that I am involved in a program that is really futuristic, is pertinent and meaningful, and is going to change the way we teach."

NASA support. The college has received, and continues to enjoy, enthusiastic support by NASA administrators, educators, scientists, and engineers.

Further development. BioBLAST is still under development; therefore, Project staff has only begun to assess its impact. As beta testing continues, they will be better able to understand its contributions.

DIFFICULTIES (ANTICIPATED AND UNANTICIPATED)

Developing accurate, realistic simulations. Difficulties arise in trying to develop fully functional simulations that address current research areas. The availability of scientific data is not consistent. In some cases, the research is underway and the data are either not yet published or incomplete. Another problem is that multiple solutions are being researched simultaneously, and NASA's approach to advanced life-support systems is evolving simultaneously with BioBLAST development. The same reasons that make working on a current problem exciting and timely also create challenges for developing simulation models.

Technical problems. Variable levels of technology available in schools and a lack of technical support to teachers have made implementation of BioBLAST difficult in some cases. Quick resolution of problems is important because Bio-BLAST testing must be integrated into already tight class schedules. Here is an example of a technical delay in software testing that was not anticipated: A school was not able to participate in the formative testing of an early version of the BaBS simulation because the school's computers were using an out-dated version of the computer's operating system and this problem was not addressed until after the close of the academic school year.

Support of multiple levels of students. As recommended in the National Science Education Standards (National Academy of Sciences, 1996), BioBLAST promotes an inquiry-based approach to learning, which may be a novel approach for both students and teachers. Most students, once they become familiar with this approach, become actively involved in the learning process. However, students who lack the basic science and math knowledge required for successfully applying the resources and tools in this program may not be prepared for the kind of problem-solving activities presented in Bio-BLAST. Some students may need more structure and direct instruction before the material in this program will be useful to them.

COSTS

The COTF BioBLAST development team includes a project manager/lead designer, two programmers/instructional designers, a graphic designer, three curriculum writers, a Web master, a desktop publisher, and part-time participation by video, editing, and copyright specialists. The extended design team includes scientific and technical experts from NASA, outside consultants who contributed specific projects, technical expertise, and content material, and a team of teachers, who review and test materials as they are created. The software and all related materials will be completed by April of 1998. This project will have taken 30 months to complete. The total cost of supporting the 2.5 years of design, development, and formative evaluation of this project has been approximately 1.5 million dollars.

CONTACT INFORMATION

Laurie Ruberg, Ph.D., Senior Instructional Designer, Project Manager
John A. Baro, Ph.D., Programmer/Instructional Designer, Assistant Project Manager
NASA Classroom of the Future, CET Building
Wheeling Jesuit University
316 Washington Avenue
Wheeling, WV 26003
(304) 243-2388
http://www.cotf.edu

BLUFORD COMMUNICATIONS MAGNET

GOALS OF TECHNOLOGY PROGRAM

- To integrate communications skills into all curriculum areas
- To maximize student achievement within a climate of high expectations
- To use Paideia instruction to enhance student communication skills
- To prepare students to be lifelong learners

KEYWORDS

- Communications
- Cooperative learning
- Paideia

LOCATION

Bluford Communications Magnet School
Guilford County Schools
1901 Tuscaloosa Street
Greensboro, NC 27401

DESCRIPTION OF SCHOOL AND COMMUNITY

- Grades K-5
- Approximately 450 students and 33 teachers
- Facility is approximately 35 years old
- This innercity school located in southeast Greensboro serves students from throughout the county Approximately 55% of Bluford's students live within the school's two attendance zones; the other 45% attend as part of the magnet program

♦ Approximately 60% of Bluford's students are African American, 35% are Caucasian, and fewer
than 5% are of other races. About 37% of students
qualify for free or reduced lunch

DESCRIPTION OF PROGRAM

Learners are enabled, through communications and technology, to become active participants in the learning process
and are taught to use technology as a tool for developing basic academic skills, critical thinking, and the interpersonal
skills needed to work in a collaborative environment. The
staff believes in the importance of student acquisition and application of basic skills and the ability to communicate
knowledge and ideas with others. Special emphases are
placed on reading, writing, listening, speaking, communication through performance, and the critical thinking skills that
propel the process of communication. Communication skills
are integrated into activities such as telecommunications,
desktop publishing, video production, amateur radio broadcasting, and multimedia presentation.

Bluford students are taught the writing process beginning in kindergarten and use computers for word processing
and publishing. A variety of writing software (including Kid
Pix, Kids' Works, Microsoft Works, Storybook Weaver, and
the Ultimate Writing Center) is used at all grade levels to
publish poems, stories, newspapers, letters, and books. Students' work appears in the student newspaper and literary
magazine, in e-mail projects with other schools, on the
school's Internet homepage, and is read at assemblies and on
the daily closed-circuit television program. In addition to the
emphasis on writing skills, the program focuses on oral communication skills. Students produce a daily closed-circuit
television program that utilizes a fifth grade production crew
and on-camera performances of students from throughout
the school.

Paideia instructional methods also incorporate communication skills with seminars and coached projects. Seminars
encourage all students to participate in discussions and to develop their reasoning and self-expression. Coached projects
permit students to make the decisions in developing materi-

als that have real-world usefulness. The school places an early emphasis on reading with both a Reading Recovery program and with community service volunteers from the neighboring high school targeting first grade students.

SPECIAL OUTCOMES, RESULTS, AND ACCOMPLISHMENTS

♦ Received State Board of Education recognition for Exemplary Academic Growth—with Distinction

♦ End-of-grade test scores that are well above system average help recruit new students to the program

♦ Bluford is one of three schools promoted by LEA for Governor's Programs of Excellence in Education recognition

♦ Internet links in 24-station computer lab, media center, and fourth and fifth grade classrooms provide students with skills and resources

♦ An amateur radio station is integrated into a communications theme with special emphasis on fifth grade social studies curriculum

♦ Students start to learn French in kindergarten

♦ Paideia instruction methods are used at all grade levels with teachers receiving training through the National Paideia Center

♦ Coached student projects in multimedia, video, desktop publishing are done

♦ A cooperative link with local colleges and universities is in place

♦ Student work is displayed in an annual literary magazine and on the school's Internet homepage

♦ The school received the 1998 North Carolina Governor's Programs of Excellence in Education Award

DIFFICULTIES (ANTICIPATED AND UNANTICIPATED)

At present, magnet programs in the district await the results of a major redistricting plan and decisions on the role that magnet schools will play in the future.

THINGS TO CONSIDER

- ◆ Faculty members need an ongoing commitment to professional development
- ◆ New faculty may have difficulty adjusting to the pace and expectations of the staff and administration. They will likely require mentoring, support, and additional professional development and time

COSTS

The school receives approximately $12,500 in special magnet funds annually. However, in the 1997-98 school year, the LEA has provided a computer lab upgrade, a fiber-optic Internet link, classroom CD-ROM reading centers, and a networked color printer.

Two special positions at the school (Communications Specialist and French teacher) require ongoing commitment of funds.

CONTACT INFORMATION

Jeff Tudor
Communications Specialist
Phone: (336) 370-8120
Fax: (336) 370-8124
e-mail: jtudor@guilford.k12.nc.us

BUILDING A COMPUTER GRAPHICS LAB

GOALS OF TECHNOLOGY PROGRAM

- To have students gain effective problem-solving skills
- To provide staff development courses
- To enable students to gain peer-teaching skills
- To have students develop multimedia projects

KEYWORDS

- Animation
- Graphics
- MIDI
- Modeling
- Multimedia
- Video

LOCATION

South Burlington Schools
550 Dorset Street
South Burlington, VT 05403

DESCRIPTION OF SCHOOL AND COMMUNITY

- Grades 9–12 (some work is also done with elementary and middle school students)
- Approximately 865 students and 104 teachers (high school)
- The Imaging Lab is a computer graphics lab that is totally supported by gifts, grants, and donations. It contains Amiga computer systems for 2-D animation and Silicon Graphics workstations for

high-end computing. Software from Alias/Wave-front, SoftImage, and 3D Studio Max is utilized

♦ South Burlington is a suburban school providing education to students who are essentially white middle-class Americans. The school system also serves other surrounding districts that do not have their own high schools

DESCRIPTION OF PROGRAM

The program utilizes animation as a "hook" to get students, faculty, and townspeople involved with computers. Courses on 2-D, 3-D, modeling, animation, and presentation programs are available. Strong Video Production and MIDI music components are also available concurrently. The lab survives with gifts, grants, donations, and the sale of students' products. Students are utilized for teaching, and they have conducted in-service programs for faculty, staff, and administrators of the district. Beyond an academic course called "Electronic Arts," students also conduct an afterschool program for at-risk kids with the Police Department, an evening course for townspeople through the Recreation Department, and a summer program for a local university.

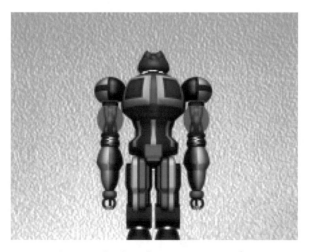

3D Studio Max "Robot." Artist Raymond Bergeron.
© Imaging Lab, South Burlington High School

For animation projects, students begin by using old Amiga 2000 systems running a program called Deluxe Paint 4. If they wish, they may remain at that level for the entire Electronic Arts course. Students who wish may move up to more sophisticated levels that include Pentium systems running 3D Studio Max. They also have the option to work on Silicon Graphics workstations. These high-end machines run both Alias/Wavefront and SoftImage, the current selection of software for the entertainment industry.

All of these machines and software were donated by the manufactures or were purchased with the help of the sale of student products. The students have put together a "demo" reel of their work and that forms the basis for approaching businesses and grantors. Students currently teach in-service training for teachers, administrators, and townspeople. They also teach a course for Saint Michael's College. Their work has been featured in national publications and has been sold locally. They have presented nationally at Princeton (The New Jersey Education Summit) and MIT and at many technology conferences nationally.

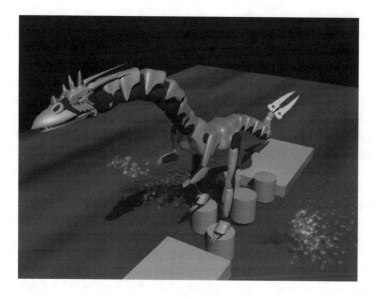

Alias/Wavefront "Dragon." Artist Todd Cox.
© Imaging Lab, South Burlington High School

The MIDI lab is a new venture this year. The corporate sponsors are Contois Music and Yamaha Music Corporation. The school is excited about this new venture wherein students now write the music for the individuals' animations, logos, and demo reels.

A complete music facility, including an electronic music teacher, will combine the business community and the educational community in a single in-school program. Hardware and software for each of the MIDI lab stations includes:

- Gateway 2000 (200 MHz)
- Yamaha CBX-K1XG keyboard
- Yamaha QY 700 board for music composition and to layer tracks
- MD4 multitrack recorder and mixing board Music Time and Music Track Pro for sequencing and composition printing

SPECIAL OUTCOMES, RESULTS, AND ACCOMPLISHMENTS

Students leave the course with skills that permit them to immediately gain employment in the field of graphics. They also produce a personal "demo reel" of their work that many students have used as a portfolio for college entrance. Students have been recruited by some of the top colleges in the country. They have been asked to present nationally at SIGGRAPH (the world's largest computer graphics trade show) and other technology conferences. They have also presented at MIT and Princeton. Last year, a lab student was named second runner-up in the national Young Technology Leaders Competition at the National Educational Computing Conference in Seattle. The lab has won the prestigious "The Road Ahead Grant" from Bill Gates and the Microsoft Corporation. Other grant sources include The Henderson Foundation Grant, Digital Equipment Corporation, Silicon Graphics Inc. Model Schools Grant, AutoDesk, and NewTek grants. For the last two years, the lab director was named the Technology and Learning State Teacher of the Year. He has also been named Vermont District Teacher of the Year and is listed in *Who's Who in American Education.*

DIFFICULTIES (ANTICIPATED AND UNANTICIPATED)

Funding is a continuing concern. The scheduling of students and the availability of teachers is also a problem.

COSTS

Amiga Video Toaster $5,000
                    (The rest of the material has been donated)

CONTACT INFORMATION

Tim Comolli, Imaging Lab Director
(802) 652-7058
(802) 652-7013 (Fax)
e-mail: Comollitd@aol.com or Tim@sbsd1.sburl.k12.vt.us
http://www.sburl.k12.vt.us/sbhs/imagelab/

CASTING THE NETS FOR TECHNOLOGY PARTNERSHIPS

GOALS OF TECHNOLOGY PROGRAM

- To encourage and support educators, students, and community partners in promoting collaborative use of technology

KEYWORDS

- Adult education
- Cooperative learning
- Senior citizens

LOCATION

Atchison Middle School
USD 409
301 N. 5th Street
Atchison, KS 66002

DESCRIPTION OF SCHOOL AND COMMUNITY

- Grades 6–8 with 415 students and 30 teachers
- Facility is 83 years old
- Atchison is a rural community with high unemployment. Fifty-two percent of the students are from low socioeconomic environments. There is a 20% African American population and less than 1% other minorities

DESCRIPTION OF PROGRAM

The Casting the Nets for Community Partnerships program has established several collaborative projects with community partners since 1993. The local AppleNet User Group and The Road Ahead Team at Atchison Middle School were recipients of funding from Apple Computer User Group Connection and Microsoft to reach reluctant technology users, especially females who represent an at-risk population in areas of math, science, and technology.

The AppleNet Community Center Lab, in a classroom at Atchison Middle School, provides local and global networking. Partnerships have been established with Girl Scouts of the USA, Adult Learning Center, Shepherd's Center Senior Citizen Program, and Benedictine College Education Program. Each community group has established projects and uses the AppleNet Lab on a continuing basis.

The Casting the Nets for Community Partnerships program allows multigenerational use of technology across ability grouping and curriculum areas. Leaders guide student learning in online communications, camera and video production, desktop publishing, and the use of multimedia software. Examples of partnership projects include:

- Senior citizen anthologies in print and online
- Technology badges for Brownies, Girl Scouts, and Cadets
- Multimedia stacks in various content areas, including biographies
- Desktop publishing scrapbook for graduates of the GED program
- NET (New Explorations in Technology) after-school study club
- Cable broadcasts spotlighting student success in the community
- "Write On" project collaboration with Benedictine College
- ThinkQuest Riverbend Web Museum and local workshop hosts

SPECIAL OUTCOMES, RESULTS, AND ACCOMPLISHMENTS

One of the greatest achievements of community partnerships and student interaction is being able to witness the boost to individual self-esteem. Multiple partnerships with the Shepherd's Center, Project Concern, Adult Education, Girl Scouts, the Amelia Earhart Birthplace, and Benedictine College continue to promote life-long learning. A technology graduate level class and four courses for pre-service teachers are being taught at the middle school site.

DIFFICULTIES (ANTICIPATED AND UNANTICIPATED)

District technology plans must present a clear direction for implementation in the classroom. With every change in administration, technology emphasis shifts toward other goals. There is always a need to upgrade hardware, maintain labs and networks, and upgrade software. The provision of faculty and staff training is essential for student success. Historically, training has been the missing link in technology planning. Teaching teams can become change agents, but the successful use of technology in the curriculum requires that all participants understand the goals and make decisions accordingly.

THINGS TO CONSIDER

Success depends on creative innovators regardless of their expertise in using technology. A need to explore ways to manage classroom time and extracurricular projects, promote effective use of peer mentoring, formulate detailed plans, and provide feedback to all partners is an essential component in the implementation of technology partnerships. The future of such programs demands that all administrators understand the goals and make decisions accordingly.

Teams should be willing to replicate student learning for educators and other school districts, for implementation in the classroom. It is encouraging to see systemic change as a result of grassroots innovation and corporate funding. The numerous achievements and a significant rise in self-esteem for many individuals must be considered the major accomplishments.

COSTS

Hardware: $35,000
(includes 14 workstations, 1 Powerbook, presentation system, 1 digital camera, 1 scanner, 3 printers, 2 TV/VCRs, modems, 2 video cameras with tripods)

Software: $8,000
(multimedia software, telecommunications, etc.)

Training: $10,000
(workshops, seminars, conferences, graduate stipend)

CONTACT INFORMATION

Mary Van Dyke
(913) 367-5363
(913) 367-1302 (Fax)
e-mail: energy@aol.com or roadteam@journey.com

CATs: COMPOSITE TEACHING—AUTHENTIC ASSESSMENT

GOALS OF TECHNOLOGY PROGRAM

- ♦ To develop innovative teaching strategies and assessment methods for block scheduling

KEYWORDS

- ♦ Animation
- ♦ Block schedule
- ♦ Cooperative Learning
- ♦ Multimedia
- ♦ Problem solving

LOCATION

Hackettstown High School
Warren County
701 Warren Street
Hackettstown, NJ 07840

DESCRIPTION OF SCHOOL AND COMMUNITY

- ♦ Grades 9–12
- ♦ Approximately 800 students and 70 teachers
- ♦ Facility is approximately 40 years old.

DESCRIPTION OF PROGRAM

CATs is an interdisciplinary program that evolved from a need for new teaching strategies able to meet the demands of extended instructional periods and block scheduling. Block scheduling was studied at the school for two years prior to its implementation in 1996. The new scheduling model coincided with the third year of implementation of a 1.2 million dollar technology plan.

Hackettstown uses a 4x4 scheduling model. Students schedule for eight courses, four taught in the fall semester and four taught in the spring semester. Each period or block is 82 minutes long; there are no study halls. The graduation credit requirement for the class of 2000 is 140 credits. During the first year of implementation, teachers divided into two distinct groups. The larger group by far was composed of individuals who looked forward to creating initiatives using newly available technologies but who lacked specific directions for curriculum applications. The second group was composed of individuals whose comfort levels were based on a traditional teacher-centered, textbook-oriented (42-minute period) curriculum. Their teaching style was largely convergent in nature. These teachers covered facts, having students memorize material rather than uncover facts through experience and applications (i.e., divergent teaching). This group was characterized by an early rush to the copy machine in order to expand teaching materials for longer instructional periods.

Administrators saw an immediate need for and opportunity to change traditional staff training patterns while developing new instructional strategies and assessment techniques. CATs was one of several initiatives that came out during this time. It mixed interdisciplinary teaching and learning, peer tutoring for technology, and teaming. CATs provided a practical curricular application at a comfort level with which staff could live.

In the CATs method, teachers form a composite team from related disciplines. They brainstorm a practical problem-solving scenario, which lends itself to open-ended multiple solutions. The team then sets corresponding instructional goals and student outcomes for tasks related to solving the scenario. Technology is used as a key to link related content areas such as a math/science technology interface (testing, evaluating, presenting data) or language arts interface (research and presentation using desktop publishing, animation, design, and illustration software). Rubrics are designed for specific purposes (technology presentation, research, cooperative learning, etc.) and can be tailored as an evaluation tool to involve the students in their own assessment. As in any cooperative learning environment group, members play to each other's strengths. In these cases, team members learned both how to use technology and how it applied in other areas. A real-life, work-based environment was created for both students and staff (see the "Athletic Shoe Scenario" example on page).

SPECIAL OUTCOMES, RESULTS, AND ACCOMPLISHMENTS

- ◆ Traditional curriculum boundaries were crossed
- ◆ More knowledge transfer occurred from one discipline to another
- ◆ Staff ability to use technology rose through a more casual and relaxed atmosphere
- ◆ Expensive media and computer equipment became multipurpose and was used more often
- ◆ Interactive multimedia presentations became more commonplace.
- ◆ More opportunities for authentic assessment involving technology were created
- ◆ Elevated levels of self-esteem through pride of accomplishment, for both students and staff, were observed

DIFFICULTIES (ANTICIPATED AND UNANTICIPATED)

Scheduling planning time seemed to be the most common complaint. Teachers needed more contact time with each other. This was addressed in part by building administrators, allowing time during faculty meetings and in-service days for team members to meet.

The school's block schedule is set up so that each teacher has a daily 82-minute related educational activity (REA) period.

ATHLETIC SHOE SCENARIO

SCENARIO:

You are a Cadkey salesman who is out of a job because Cadkey's reputation for quality has created a demand for the product eliminating the need for a sales force.

Instructions:

You decide to use your knowledge of Cadkey to design, test, and market an athletic shoe. Develop a complete set of working drawings of your shoe.

GRADING:

Design Brief	100 pts.
Working Drawings	100 pts.

TIME FRAME:

I.	Ideation—Brainstorming:	2 Days
II.	Identify Project Goals and Conduct Research:	3 Days
III.	Develop and Test Prototype:	7 Days
IV.	Report Results:	1 Day

INTEGRATED SUBJECT MATTER

PHYSICS

APPLICATION:

QUESTION # 1:

A man, standing barefoot, weighs 180 pounds with a total area of both feet equaling 68 square inches. Calculate the pressure he exerts on the ground normally and when standing on one foot.

ANSWER:

180 lbs./68 square in. = pressure exerted on the ground when standing on two feet = 2.647 lbs. per square inch.

180 lbs./34 square in. = pressure exerted on the ground when standing on one foot = 5.294 lbs. per square inch.

THINGS TO CONSIDER

The interdisciplinary learning modules were often broadened beyond their original scope and sequence as student and teacher interest in technology applications increased.

Commitment from building supervision and administration for flexibility in planning time and for use of specialized computer graphics labs is needed.

An educational philosophy is required that transcends traditional curriculum boundaries and realizes the benefit of applied, work-based learning through composite teaching (common knowledge transfer—career and occupational infusion—authentic assessment.)

COSTS

Hardware: Existing computer labs in business, technology, and the media center are used. Because the initiative crosses other disciplines, expensive equipment that may not normally be available under traditional curriculum boundaries is maximized and staff from related content areas see the benefit of peer coaching. The lab used most extensively is the school's CADD lab which runs a nonnetworked Windows platform. Approximate cost for 12 IBM clones, specialty printers, press pen plotters, and furniture is $32,000.

Apple Quick Take digital camera $800
Nonlinear video editing system with titling and special effects $9,000
HP 4C scanner $1,000

Software: Microsoft Office Suite is networked on our LAN and available in every classroom. Cost varies by the number of network users. Other software includes SmartSound, Autodesk's 3-D Studio Max, Adobe Photoshop, Cadkey, DataCad, Ray Dream Studio, PhotoMorph, Gryphon Morph, and Fractal Design's Painter. Approximate cost $4,500.

CONTACT INFORMATION

Roy A. Huchel
District Technology Supervisor
(908) 850-6535
(908) 852-6214 (Fax)
e-mail: rhuchellab@aol.com

Robert Redmon
Technology teacher
(908) 852-8150
e-mail: caddtcrh@aol.com
http://www/gti.net/hackboe

CD-ROM RECORDING: IT WILL WORK IN YOUR CURRICULUM

GOALS OF TECHNOLOGY PROGRAM

- To implement technology into the core curriculum
- To make history exciting and interesting
- To place students into a situation where they are engaged learners
- To focus on a finished product that would motivate and drive the students
- To teach the students to orchestrate a complex project

KEYWORDS

- Cooperative learning
- History
- Multimedia

LOCATION

Lakes Middle School
Coeur d'Alene School District
311 North 10th Street
Coeur d'Alene, ID 83814

DESCRIPTION OF SCHOOL AND COMMUNITY

- Grades 6–8
- Approximately 1,050 students and 50 teachers
- Lakes Middle School is located in the town of Coeur d'Alene in northern Idaho. Students come from a wide range of socioeconomic backgrounds. Employment is mostly logging, mining, and tourism.

DESCRIPTION OF PROGRAM

Students are divided into groups of four. Each group of students is responsible for creating a history CD-ROM covering early migration across the Bering Strait through the Civil War. These complex projects take the entire school year and culminate in the burning of a history CD-ROM for each member of each group. The group has 24 students and generates six different CDs. At the beginning of a new unit, the teacher hands a folder to each group. Within the folder is an outline describing the subjects to research. He also includes a student evaluation form used for grading, as well as a flow chart showing how the project should be assembled. The students are required to include pictures or artwork, as well as a written report for each subject. They are also encouraged to add audio, animation, and video. (See the Sample Unit on page 93.)

Each student has a job within the group. The teacher allows the students to choose which job they prefer. The options are art director, research director, copy director, and project director. Responsibilities are as follows: The art director is responsible for collecting and making decisions on which graphics are to be used within the project; the research director gives out assignments as to who will research what for the unit and where it might be found; the copy director is responsible for making sure all reports are completed and placed in the project; and the project director actually builds the interactive project in the computer and reports to the teacher on the project's progress.

All students write reports and sharing of jobs becomes a part of the group function. The teacher also lectures to cover material and tests to check for understanding. The CD-ROM projects are very attractive and could pass as being created by a professional authoring business.

SPECIAL OUTCOMES, RESULTS, AND ACCOMPLISHMENTS

The students become so engaged in the project that many come to class to work before school, after school, and, if the teacher would let them, during lunch. Students have little patience for lazy workers who turn in poor work or no work at all.

The teacher expected to find that low achievers improved their performance and this did occur. The biggest surprise, however, was how the high achievers took off and performed when not held back. Too often in the classroom students are stifled with boring worksheets and mundane lectures. When given a chance to let their "creative juices" flow, it is astounding what they can achieve. Students learned without even knowing they were learning. One student yelled out in class, "Hey, who has that report on nullification?" It just became a part of the daily routine.

In a project such as this, students will often go back and revisit a section they are past, just to do it a little better. The students are also working with the most sophisticated software on the market (e.g., Adobe Premiere, Photoshop, Macromedia Director, Sound Edit 16, and Fractal Design Painter). They use Macintosh computers, the Radius Video Vision Studio video capture board, as well as scanners, digital cameras, Dream Writer key pads, video camera, and CD-ROM writers. The group does not focus on the technology but rather uses it as a tool to create the projects. Students have fun designing their group's CD cover, along with credits. It is a project that keeps on teaching, as opposed to a stack of worksheets that fly into the dumpster on the last day of school. Students have approached the teacher during the summer to tell him how much they enjoy viewing their historical CD. Students also learn to work in groups to coordinate complex projects.

DIFFICULTIES (ANTICIPATED AND UNANTICIPATED)

Drawbacks were the large amount of time required to run the technology and actually build the project. This, along with downtime from computer failures, was frustrating. At times, the teacher just wanted to stop the project and lecture or hand out worksheets. Not as much material is covered, but the students will retain more of what they learn through project-based learning. Less can be more. The teacher noted that he once gave a 50-question test covering the Civil War. The students asked to have five minutes to review their notes for the test. At the end of the five minutes, a student asked,

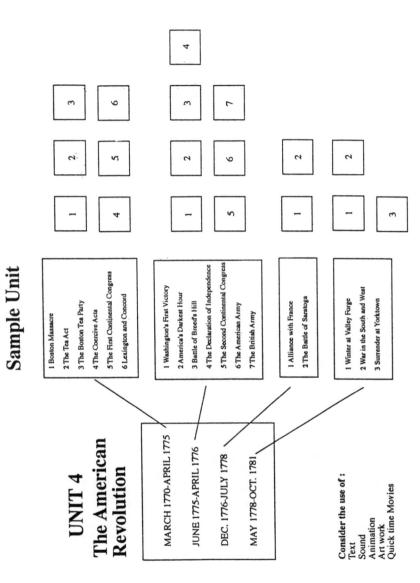

Sample Unit

**UNIT 4
The American Revolution**

Boxes	
1 Boston Massacre	
2 The Tea Act	
3 The Boston Tea Party	
4 The Coercive Acts	
5 The First Continental Congress	
6 Lexington and Concord	

1 Washington's First Victory
2 America's Darkest Hour
3 Battle of Breed's Hill
4 The Declaration of Independence
5 The Second Continental Congress
6 The American Army
7 The British Army

1 Alliance with France
2 The Battle of Saratoga

1 Winter at Valley Forge
2 War in the South and West
3 Surrender at Yorktown

MARCH 1770-APRIL 1775

JUNE 1775-APRIL 1776

DEC. 1776-JULY 1778

MAY 1778-OCT. 1781

Consider the use of :
Text
Sound
Animation
Art work
Quick time Movies

"Can we hurry up and take the test before I forget all this information?" In contrast, when the group reviewed one of the history CDs they had created, the entire class sang along with the song "The Battle of New Orleans."

Another drawback is that the teacher must keep an eye out for lazy students. Project-based learning leaves a door open for the lazy student to be a slacker. Although students will argue within groups, they should not be allowed to change groups under any circumstance. Also, the teacher should not resolve their arguments unless they become unmanageable and detrimental to the group. The high cost of the technology is another hindrance when attempting to implement technology into the curriculum.

THINGS TO CONSIDER

If you really want to implement a program like this, you can. However, you must be willing to do a lot of work. The rewards are tremendous.

COSTS

Grants paid for almost all of the equipment used on this project. The lab has about $70,000 worth of technology in it. At today's prices, a lab could be outfitted for much less.

CONTACT INFORMATION

Mike Clabby
Computer graphics and history teacher
Phone: (208) 769-0769
e-mail: clabby@ior.com

COMPUTER CAMP

GOALS OF TECHNOLOGY PROGRAM

- To introduce inner-city high school students to current computer technology

KEYWORDS

- Computer camp
- Computer technology

LOCATION

Cleveland City School District
Administration Building
1380 E. 6th Street
Cleveland, Ohio 44115
(District from which students came)

Cleveland State University
1983 E. 24th Street
Cleveland, Ohio 44115
(Location where Computer Camp was held)

DESCRIPTION OF SCHOOL AND COMMUNITY

- Grades 1–12
- Approximately 76,518 students and 5,000 teachers in district
- Facility (used by the Computer Camp): Computer labs at Cleveland State University
- Cleveland is a large metropolitan area with a diverse population

DESCRIPTION OF PROGRAM

A 10-day computer camp was held at Cleveland State University for 60 innercity high school students from Cleveland. Three groups of 20 students were formed, and students stayed with the same group of 20 students for the duration of the camp. Each group was given the name of a famous computer scientist (names such as Hopper, Turing, and Babbage were used).

A total of 12 instructors taught in three computer labs at CSU, with two instructors and two assistants working with 20 students. Students had their own computers.

On the first day of the camp, a brief orientation was held, followed by a general introduction to computers. The general introduction included computer basics, such as the role of people, hardware, and software in a computer system. Campers also looked at the inner workings of a computer after the various components were explained.

After this general introduction to computers, the curriculum was divided into three parts: computer skills, the Internet, and programming in C. In the computer skills segment, groups briefly discussed file management (e.g., saving files and creating directories) and assigned short exercises using DOS. They also discussed Windows, Write, Paintbrush, and PowerPoint. Students demonstrated their creativity as they made their own slide shows using PowerPoint. The students' slide shows revealed what they learned and enjoyed at the computer camp and what they planned to do after graduation from high school.

In the Internet session, students were introduced to the World Wide Web and Netscape. Students visited the White House and foreign countries as they surfed the Internet. Their major project in this session was to create personal Web pages using HTML. The campers developed many outstanding pages, some of which included photos.

In the C-programming session, leaders taught students the rudiments of programming. This was the most difficult session to conduct because it required more instruction than the others. Creating software, as opposed to using software, definitely turned on a group of the more technically inclined students who appreciated the power of programming. The main project was the creation of a modified version of Pac-Man using the graphics library of C.

SPECIAL OUTCOMES, RESULTS, AND ACCOMPLISHMENTS

The students completed anonymous evaluations at the conclusion of the camp. The results were very positive. The statement that students agreed with most was, "I will probably use the skills and knowledge I gained from this camp later in my life."

Also, based on observations of the small groups of 20, the students were genuinely excited about using the computer to create their unique presentations. Hopefully, this enthusiasm for using computer technology carried over into their lives after they left the Camp.

DIFFICULTIES (ANTICIPATED AND UNANTICIPATED)

Although each group of 20 students had two instructors and two assistants, a few more instructors and assistants would result in even more personal attention. This would be especially important if there were students who presented special challenges.

COSTS

Total cost was approximately $38,000. Approximately $8,000 was used for startup expenses, with the remaining $30,000 for operational expenses. Included in the startup expenses were bus tickets ($1,000) to provide free transportation for the students; supplies ($4,000) such as floppy disks, folders, pads and pens, which were provided at no cost to the students; and lunches and snacks ($3,000), which were provided at no charge to the students. Included in the operational expenses were stipends for the instructors and assistants ($20,000); the overhead of lab usage ($4,000); and the administration of the camp ($6,000).

CONTACT INFORMATION

Dr. Barbara Benander, Associate Professor
(216) 687-4781 or (216) 289-8137
e-mail: bbenande@cis.csuohio.edu

DISTRIBUTED COMPUTING
WITH EMATES

GOALS OF TECHNOLOGY PROGRAM

- ♦ To develop a distributed learning environment that will enhance the educational mission of the school by providing portable computing devices to supplement the existing classroom technology

KEYWORDS

- ♦ Distributed learning
- ♦ Cooperative learning
- ♦ Laptop computers

LOCATION

Manatee High School
Manatee County
902 33rd Street Ct. W.
Bradenton, FL 34205

DESCRIPTION OF SCHOOL AND COMMUNITY

- ♦ Grades 9–12
- ♦ Approximately 2,460 students
- ♦ Approximately 127 teachers
- ♦ Original facility was built in 1927; most of the campus is newly renovated and rebuilt
- ♦ Manatee High School is located in Bradenton, Florida, south of Tampa on Florida's West Coast. The school's 2,400 students represent a diverse socioeconomic mix, and come from families that range from low- to upper-middle class. The area's major industries are tourism and agriculture

DESCRIPTION OF PROGRAM

Distributed learning extends the reach of learning beyond the classroom walls, making it possible for learning to take place any time, any where, and any place. The new student laptop from Apple Computer called the eMate dramatically increases the student-to-computer ratio and provides the much needed technology resources for students to learn to compete successfully in the twenty-first century. This program started with the principal and the technology coordinator laying the groundwork for introducing this new product to the faculty and students. As the initial effort proceeded, faculty and students quickly became the driving force for implementing this new technology into the curriculum.

One goal of the project was to determine what impact this technology would have on students who had not been successful in 9th-grade English. A special pilot study was done with eighteen 9th-grade English students who had failed the first semester of English. These students were grouped into a two-hour block for the second semester. They were each given an eMate as a writing tool for the last nine weeks of the second semester. Although they only had access to the eMates for a nine-week period, the results were incredible. The writing skills of each student increased by at least two grade levels. Students demonstrated a great sense of pride in their writing and in their accomplishments.

A second goal was to evaluate the impact of this technology in the science classroom. Thirty units and probeware were allotted to the department as a science lab. Students were able to take the eMate and probeware on field trips to collect data, make drawings, and write about their experiences. This tool became an integral component in many chemistry, biology, and physics classes. Although the school has just begun to tap into the capabilities of using the eMate in science, it has had an immediate impact on classroom instruction.

A third goal was to provide the English department with easy access to the writing tools needed for student compositions. Thirty eMates were set aside as a "floating" writing lab for the English department. Instead of sending students to the writing lab for compositions, the school brought the lab to the classroom, allowing more time for students to be productive. The eMates have a built-in security system that allows each student a personal login, thus protecting each student's work and allowing up to seven students to share an eMate. The files are easily transferred from the eMate to a desktop computer, creating a personal folder or directory for each student. A student can borrow an eMate when more time is required to finish his or her work.

In addition to the curriculum implications experienced, the eMate has also become a valuable tool for the classroom teacher. Approximately 30 teachers are actively using the eMate to produce tests, worksheets, outlines, and so forth, for their classrooms. The goal is to provide an eMate to every teacher who desires one, thereby providing an affordable, portable tool to increase the teacher's productivity.

SPECIAL OUTCOMES, RESULTS, AND ACCOMPLISHMENTS

- All but one student in the pilot study passed 9th grade English
- An increased number of students had access to technology, improving their laboratory writing and evaluative skills
- An increase in students' desire to write compositions as well as in the amount of writing they were able to do was noted
- A marked increase in innovative ideas by teachers was observed, thereby changing instructional approaches in the classroom

DIFFICULTIES (ANTICIPATED AND UNANTICIPATED)

As with the introduction of any new technology, more time is needed to fully utilize all of the capabilities of the eMate. Effective training is difficult because the product is so new and few people are truly experts at using it and troubleshooting its problems. The school also underestimated the number of power adapters needed to effectively recharge a large number of eMates.

THINGS TO CONSIDER

- ♦ Purchase enough power adapters to recharge the eMates quickly
- ♦ Students who are motivated and excited will be independent learners
- ♦ Faculty members must be willing to invest time in training and be willing to take risks

COSTS

Hardware: $9,087 or $699/8 eMates
13 additional power adapters: $325
2 8-packs of eprobes (with software): $4,000
Training: $1,100

CONTACT INFORMATION

Tina M. Barrios, Ph.D.
(941) 714-7300
(941) 741-3443 (Fax)
e-mail: Barrios_T@popmail.firn.edu

EIGHTH GRADE GENERAL MUSIC: KEYBOARD-BASED CURRICULUM

GOALS OF TECHNOLOGY PROGRAM

- ◆ To utilize the piano/keyboard technology lab as a vehicle to achieve the National Standard's goals for eighth grade classroom music in four key curricular components: singing, music history and appreciation, creating, and performing student compositions
- ◆ To individualize instruction for a spectrum of learners, from the mentally and physically challenged to the gifted student
- ◆ To create an environment that lays a foundation for the continuation of lifelong applications and appreciation of music

KEYWORDS

- ◆ Individualized instruction
- ◆ Music
- ◆ Music technology
- ◆ National Standards

LOCATION

State College Area School District
Park Forest Middle School
2180 School Drive
State College, PA 16803

Mount Nittany Middle School
656 Brandywine Drive
State College, PA 16801

DESCRIPTION OF SCHOOL AND COMMUNITY

Park Forest Middle School

- ◆ Grades 6–8
- ◆ Approximately 826 students in school and 7,366 students in district
- ◆ Approximately 75 teachers in school and 582 teachers in district
- ◆ Facility is a single floor, 29,000 sq. ft., 28-year-old structure

Mount Nittany Middle School

- ◆ Grades 6–8
- ◆ Approximately 937 students in school
- ◆ Approximately 79 teachers in school
- ◆ Facility is a two-floor, 156,000 sq. ft., 3-year-old structure

The town surrounds The Pennsylvania State University, University Park campus.

DESCRIPTION OF PROGRAM

This music program was developed to address the kinesthetic as well as aural and visual learning styles of today's middle level students who are immersed in a world of technitronics. It provides an alternative approach to traditional lecture/listening activities.

General music at the eighth-grade level is a required class that meets daily for an entire semester. The course of study was designed around four key curricular components of the National Standards for eighth grade classroom music: singing, music history and appreciation, creating, and performing, each of which is addressed through the use of the keyboard tech lab.

At the program's inception, the equipment used to outfit the lab consisted of ten simplistic electric keyboards (without headphones) and three upright, acoustic pianos. Currently, the program is in the third year of a six-year plan to upgrade and improve the lab's technology systems.

The first year's goal was to declare the eighth grade general music classroom a designated keyboard lab. This was accomplished by permanently placing the keyboards at thirteen workstations throughout the room and outfitting each keyboard with two sets of stereo headphones to encourage cooperative learning through the pairing of students at each station.

Thirteen new, MIDI, touch-sensitive, 64-note instruments have been installed. Adjustable-height tables have replaced individual desks. Five Macintosh computers with notation software and two printers are being used instead of the traditional pencil/paper manuscript.

Projections for year 6 include upgrading to six computers, allowing every two keyboards access to one monitor, and alphanumeric controls at each keyboard. In addition, instruction will be enhanced with a group controller that permits individual or group performance monitoring via headphones and microphones. Implementation of this phase of the program will coincide with a primary goal of the State College Area School District's Strategic Plan 1995–2001, which is to acquire, develop and integrate technology to enhance teaching, learning and operations at all levels in the school.

It is the mission of the district's Strategic Plan to prepare students to become lifelong learners. It is anticipated that the use of the keyboard/technology lab will provide a vehicle through which students may lay the foundation for lifelong applications and appreciation of music.

SPECIAL OUTCOMES, RESULTS, AND ACCOMPLISHMENTS

- ♦ Presenters at the 1997 Pennsylvania Music Educators Association Conference in Pittsburgh, PA (Middle School sharing session: Keyboard-based curriculum); invited to return for the 1999 conference
- ♦ Awarded the 1997 "Best Practices in Pennsylvania Arts in Education"

DIFFICULTIES (ANTICIPATED AND UNANTICIPATED)

- Too many wires!
- Faculty and staff must be aware of all budget dates for submitting and resubmitting requests for the next phase
- Replacement costs of headphones and headphone adapters

COSTS

13 Kawai X55D keyboards: $7,800
28 Sony MDR-V100 headphones: $672
5 Macintosh computers
1 Korg X3 keyboard: $1,300
14 Radio Shack headphone adapters
13 Kawai AC power adapters
8 Adjustable leg tables (leftover from library)
2 Printers (laser and dot matrix)
1 Acoustic piano (leftover from classroom)
Music Maid notation software: $28
Finale notation software: $295

CONTACT INFORMATION

Jo E. Henry (Park Forest Middle School)
8th grade music teacher
(814) 237- 5301
(814) 235-4505 (Fax)
e-mail: jeh14@scasd.k12.pa.us

Samuel Rocco (Park Forest Middle School and Mount Nittany Middle School)
7th/8th grade music teacher
e-mail: sar12@scasd.k12.pa.us

Amy McMillin (Mount Nittany Middle School)
8th grade music teacher
(814) 466-5133 school
e-mail: abm11@scasd.k12.pa.us

GLOBAL LEARNING AND OBSERVATION TO BENEFIT THE ENVIRONMENT

GOALS OF TECHNOLOGY PROGRAM

- ◆ To enable students to collect and transmit scientific data to a central data processing facility via the Internet
- ◆ To enable students to acquire information from a variety of sources
- ◆ To encourage students to collaborate with scientists and other students and communities worldwide in using the data for education and research

KEYWORDS

- ◆ Distance learning
- ◆ GLOBE
- ◆ Science
- ◆ Telecommunications

LOCATION

Enterprise Elementary School
Brevard County Public Schools
7000 Enterprise Road
Cocoa, FL 32927

The GLOBE Program
744 Jackson Place
Washington, DC 20503

DESCRIPTION OF SCHOOL AND COMMUNITY

- Grades Pre-K–5
- Approximately 900 students and 48 teachers
- Facility is 5 years old.
- Enterprise Elementary is located on the central east coast of Florida, near Kennedy Space Center in a community known as Port St. John. The area's major industries are NASA, governmental contractors, and tourism, but it also supports a growing number of businesses and light industries. The school population is approximately 92% Caucasian and 8% minority

DESCRIPTION OF PROGRAM

GLOBE (Global Learning and Observation to Benefit the Environment) is a hands-on international environmental science and education program. It links students, educators, and the scientific research community in an effort to learn more about our environment through student data collection and observation. The goals of the program are to:

- Enhance the environmental awareness of individuals throughout the world
- Contribute to scientific understanding of the Earth
- Help all students reach higher levels of achievement in science and mathematics

The GLOBE program provides extensive educational materials used to enrich the learning experience of participating students. These materials are obtained once the teacher has attended a GLOBE workshop. Materials include a wide variety of classroom and field activities to help students place their measurements in a broader context and relate their own local observations to global environmental issues.

At the GLOBE workshop, the GLOBE teacher receives a Teacher's Guide that reflects a balance between science and education. It is filled with scientific protocols and learning activities which are appropriate for both primary and secondary students. The hands-on, minds-on approach of the protocols and activities gives the students a sense of being environmental experts for their study sites.

The GLOBE-trained teacher receives a software program called MultiSpec that can be used in the classroom. MultiSpec was funded by a NASA grant, in conjunction with the Purdue Research Foundation, and allows investigation of the use of satellite imaging in an educational setting. The program was intended for use at the university level, but it has proven to be a highly motivational educational computer program at the elementary through high school level. It is now licensed through the Purdue Research Foundation for universal use.

Students in the GLOBE Program range in age from 5 to 18 years and are studying in schools throughout the world. They carry out a series of investigations that scientists have designed to gather data about the Earth and how it functions as a global system. The students use instruments and their own senses to observe the environment at multiple sites near their school. These investigations include monitoring the air, water, soil, and vegetation. They record the data they gather, save it in a permanent school data record, and then send it to the GLOBE Student Data Server using the Internet and the World Wide Web, or e-mail where the Web is not readily available.

The measurements taken by GLOBE students serve two important purposes. First, participating scientists use this data in their research programs to improve our understanding of the global environment. Second, students learn how to carry out a scientifically rigorous program of Earth observations and to use their own measurements, together with data from other GLOBE schools, as a key part of their study of environmental science. Through contact with and mentoring by scientists, the students receive feedback about the value of their data sets in world-class scientific research.

SPECIAL OUTCOMES, RESULTS, AND ACCOMPLISHMENTS

Access to scientists from the research community through the use of Web chats and e-mail will enhance the exciting and rewarding relationship that occurs between the students and the scientists. The students will receive a sense of belonging to the scientific community through their involvement with the GLOBE program.

Accessibility to their peers around the world provides students with an environmental understanding of our planet and enables them to gain an understanding of other cultures and a sense of global community.

Teachers are able to give students the opportunity to explore and communicate through the powerful and easy software that the GLOBE systems provide. It also lets the students see and interact with local and worldwide maps on which the GLOBE data is displayed.

DIFFICULTIES (ANTICIPATED AND UNANTICIPATED)

Enterprise Elementary School was fortunate to be equipped with the necessary computers and online technology when the school was built five years ago. The school was able to purchase the scientific instruments through funding provided by one of its business partners. Some schools may not be as fortunate and may have to seek funding through grants, business partners, or local industries willing to make contributions.

THINGS TO CONSIDER

+ Purchase computers with adequate memory, storage, peripheral devices, and obtain online capability
+ Faculty members must be willing to invest their time to attend the GLOBE workshop for 4 days of training
+ Purchase the scientific instrument kits for GLOBE measurements—beginning (grades K–5), intermediate (grades 6–8), or advanced (grades 9–12)

COSTS

Computer and hardware: $3,000–$10,000
Software: $500–$2,500

The Training Workshop is free (except for cost of transportation, lodging, and meals depending on where the training is held; check the GLOBE Home page, http://www.globe.gov, for location, date, and time of workshop).

Teacher's Guide and materials are free.

CONTACT INFORMATION

Brenda Dibler
(407) 633-3434
(407) 633-3438 (Fax)
e-mail: Diblerb@ees.brevard.k12.fl.us
http://www.globe.gov

GLOBAL TELECOMMUNICATIONS AND VIDEO PRODUCTION

GOALS OF TECHNOLOGY PROGRAM

- To increase student skill levels through school-to-career technology programs
- To create maximum student involvement
- To generate a self-sustaining funding base for the school-to-career technology programs

KEYWORDS

- Internet
- School-to-career
- Telecommunications
- Video

LOCATION

Mount Vernon High School
314 N. 9th
Mount Vernon, WA 98273

DESCRIPTION OF SCHOOL AND COMMUNITY

- Approximately 1,500 students in grades 9–12 and approximately 75 teachers
- School facility includes multiple buildings dating from the 1920s, with remodels and additions

♦ Mount Vernon High School is located in Skagit County, Washington. The area is noted for its agriculture (especially seeds and tulips). Situated on the I-5 corridor north of Seattle, Mount Vernon has experienced residential, retail, and commercial growth in recent years. Mount Vernon was recently designated as "The Most Livable Small Town in America." Mount Vernon High School is approximately 78% Caucasian, 20% Latino, and 2% Asian, African American, Native American

DESCRIPTION OF PROGRAM

During 1994, staff at Mount Vernon High School recognized the importance of digital telecommunications (voice, video, and data) in their students' futures. What was needed was a way to generate a powerful school-to-career telecommunications program on a modest funding base. For both educational and economic reasons, it was determined to maximize the involvement of students as workers in developing the program. Under this framework, two key programs were developed: Global Telecommunications and Video Production. Each of these programs has reached its targets in the areas of student involvement and fiscal sustainability.

Global Telecommunications began with a 56K link via existing Category 5 wire to a small classroom serving English as a Second Language students. A six-station Internet Lab was wired and configured by the students. The curriculum focus in this area was basic HTML, along with e-mail, Web research, word processing, keyboarding, and fundamental language arts. Limited English students thrived on the Internet, and word soon spread among the general student population about the kinds of learning opportunities available in the connected classroom.

In discussing what to do with a one-time, per pupil technology allotment from the state, staff identified expanding the data network as a key goal. Fiber-optic links were established between six buildings, and hubs and patch panels were installed at each location. Students assisted staff and professional vendors in each phase of the design, installation, and configuration of this project. The original lab was expanded to 30 workstations and all of the original hardware and software was upgraded.

From this foundation, Global Telecommunications has grown into a two-semester sequence with emphasis on Web authoring, network administration, software consulting, and digital graphics. Students do commercial-grade work for local businesses, higher education, and governmental agencies. The program has succeeded in generating significant grant and partnership support, and students have obtained career opportunities through skills developed in the program.

Also dating from 1994, a powerful Video Production program has taken shape from very modest fiscal beginnings. Early that year, a local businessman donated a surplus Commodore Amiga to a high school art teacher. That equipment was refurbished and outfitted with video capture and editing capabilities. A new Power Macintosh was added to the class, and students began learning how to produce and edit videos.

Although staff, students, and community members were interested in the benefits of student video production, substantial school district budgets were not available for that purpose. So a "bootstrapping" model was adopte and students made a senior video. The senior video was sold at a profit to support the program. Students took on other video production work (such as developing public service announcements), with the resulting fees being reinvested in the program.

Within two years, the program had not only managed to sustain itself fiscally, but indeed was experiencing rapid growth. Mount Vernon High School student-produced public service announcements have appeared nationally on cable channels such as MTV, ESPN, and F/X. These videos focus on issues of concern to teens such as smoking and teen pregnancy.

Governmental, not-for-profit, and public health agencies have been generous in their support of the program because they view the student video productions as an effective means to communicate a positive message to teens. Students are also enjoying commercial career opportunities derived from their video production skills.

SPECIAL OUTCOMES, RESULTS, AND ACCOMPLISHMENTS

- Students have learned valuable career skills while building their own programs
- Quality educational video and Web presentations have been developed
- Student work has achieved recognition through broadcasts, conferences, and site tours by educational leaders

DIFFICULTIES (ANTICIPATED AND UNANTICIPATED)

Bootstrapping an educational technology program is similar to launching a new business. It takes a lot of hard work by everyone involved, and it is a year or two before the most significant results become apparent. These programs face any number of fiscal, technical, and organizational hurdles at the outset. It takes visionary, determined efforts to stay on course through the initial phase, where the workload is more evident than the outcome. Staff and student burnout is a major risk in such bootstrapping scenarios.

THINGS TO CONSIDER

- Focus on projects with high student appeal at the outset
- Look for an early "win" to keep everyone's spirits up
- Staff need to lead, but they also need to delegate as much as possible to students
- Look for community support and involvement to keep the program on track over the long run

COSTS

Hardware: $35,000 initially
              (over $100,000 added in three years)
Software: $ 2,000 initially
              (over $25,000 added in three years)

Training: $ 2,000 initially
(staff now provide training for other locations)

CONTACT INFORMATION

Robert Bunge
2811 Ontario
Bellingham, WA 98226
(253) 922-6697
e-mail: rbunge@esd189.wednet.edu

GRADE 1 TECHIEECOLOGISTS

GOALS OF TECHNOLOGY PROGRAM

- ◆ To bring traditional studies to life through the use of technology
- ◆ To integrate technology effectively into a primary class
- ◆ To help students learn to use technologies to enhance learning

KEYWORDS

- ◆ Curriculum integration
- ◆ Multimedia
- ◆ Science
- ◆ Telecommunications

LOCATION

Worcester Country School
PO Box 1006
508 S. Main Street
Berlin, MD 21811

DESCRIPTION OF SCHOOL AND COMMUNITY

- ◆ Grades preschool–12
- ◆ Approximately 460 students and 50 teachers
- ◆ Worcester Country School is an independent college preparatory school in a rural/resort community. Students come from a four-county, two-state area on the Delmarva Peninsula

DESCRIPTION OF PROGRAM

Celeste Bunting, a teacher with over 20 years of experience working with grade 1 students, knows how to turn her students on to science. Over the years, she has worked with her 6- and 7-year-olds to establish a children's garden and a bird sanctuary outside the grade 1 classroom windows. She has brought a love of science, the environment, and now technology to her students.

Grade 1 students call themselves the TechieEcologists because they are caretakers of our environment and use technology to help them. With their bird and butterfly scopes, they watch out the window to see what birds and butterflies are visiting their feeders and which birds and butterflies are interested in what types of berries on the bushes and trees that have been planted over the years by first graders. The students take turns recording the information in Microsoft Works on their classroom computers, describing the type of bird, the bird's beak, the color of the bird, and any other interesting information. This bird journal is kept throughout the school year. (Information on butterflies is not kept in the journal, but is used for other projects.)

In the computer lab, students draw pictures of their birds (using Kid Pix Studio), add bird call sounds, and save their work for a class slide show on birds and bird calls. They also use the drawn pictures of birds to create a bird guide featuring information about their favorite birds. On the Internet, they participate in Project Feederwatch and the Journey North program. They are also involved with programs of the Institute of Chemical Education (ICE) at the University of Wisconsin.

Some of the ideas for the project come from the students. For example, after seeing a video of cranes "dancing," one student who loved to dance, suggested that the class learn how to dance just like the cranes. She volunteered to write the instructions for the dance on the computer and print them for everyone. After the instructions were printed, the students went outside and learned the dance under the direction of this young choreographer. The teacher filmed the dancing and asked the students what they wanted to do with the film. "Let's put it into our computer," they decided. The teacher didn't know how to put video into the computer, but she said, "I'm sure it can be done." The computer teacher came to the rescue. What was created was a presentation that contained bird drawings, bird descriptions, birdcalls, the amazing crane dance, a short video of their little bird sanctuary, and a quiz. Because some of the class bird projects involved interacting with schools in Central and South America, the students also wanted to add some phrases in Español. With the assistance of Spanish instructors Señora Rauch and Señora Caine, the students copied Spanish phrases into the program. "It was quite a job putting all this together," commented teacher Celeste Bunting, "but it is something these students will never forget. Like me, they have the feeling that if you can think of something the computer should do for you, it can do it. We only have to find out how."

A visit to this classroom is indeed a unique experience. It is difficult to avoid telling the TechieEcologists what birds are on your lifetime bird list. They know their birds and will do the birdcalls for your favorite. Did you know, for example, that the OvenBird says "Teacher" and that you can hear it on their computers?

SPECIAL OUTCOMES, RESULTS, AND ACCOMPLISHMENTS

Students develop a lifelong love of science and the environment through this project. They learn that the computer can be used to find, collect, record, and present information.

The teacher and the elementary computer specialist work closely together to help the little TechieEcologists and have developed excellent templates and lessons that accompany this course.

DIFFICULTIES (ANTICIPATED AND UNANTICIPATED)

The only problem with this project is that all parents want their children to become grade 1 TechieEcologists. The school has solved that difficulty by having teachers switch classes (the school has two sections of grade 1) for science and social studies. This works well, because the social studies teacher, Cheryl Marshall, has her own dynamic work going with the grade 1 social studies curriculum.

THINGS TO CONSIDER

The most important ingredients in the success of a project such as this are the teacher and the willingness of the school system to incorporate an extensive project such as this into the science curriculum. While the school system must approve, the teacher must be willing to give time well beyond the regular school day. Learning to use the software programs, teaming with Spanish and computer teachers, making online partner connections, checking for appropriate Internet sites, editing output, and figuring out how to use technology as a tool in primary science education is not a simple job. It is, however, most rewarding.

As for software, word processing and paint software get the project started nicely. Other software relating to bird studies, an Internet browser, and a presentation program make the project even more exciting.

COSTS

There are no additional costs for this project. The students need access to a classroom computer and possibly a school computer lab. Bird feed, bird scopes, and plants for the sanctuary are covered through an annual birdseed sale to parents.

CONTACT INFORMATION

Dr. Merle Marsh
Head of the Lower School
(410) 641-3575
(410) 641-3586 (Fax)
e-mail: marsh@shore.intercom.net or merlem@aol.com

GREENWICH COUNTRY DAY SCHOOL'S MUSIC TECHNOLOGY PROGRAM

GOALS OF TECHNOLOGY PROGRAM

- To provide students with an unique contemporary platform for the development of musical talent
- To allow students to learn about music theory, composition, and the elements of music in their own language

KEYWORDS

- MIDI
- Multimedia
- Music technology

LOCATION

The Greenwich Country Day School
PO Box 623, Old Church Road
Greenwich, CT 06836-0623

DESCRIPTION OF SCHOOL AND COMMUNITY

- Grades Nursery–9
- Coeducational independent day school with 800 students and 116 faculty members
- The school was founded in 1926

DESCRIPTION OF PROGRAM

Music Technology offers students the opportunity to learn the art of computer-assisted music sequencing using state-of-the art synthesizers and computers. This exciting hands-on approach to teaching the elements of music has become a popular element of Greenwich Country Day School's music program. Students come to the lab to learn how to digitally record, edit, playback, and store original compositions, as they also improve their technical skills in music.

Beginning in grades five and six, all GCDS students study Music Technology as a component of their required computer technology program. In grades seven through nine, Music Technology may be elected as a trimester arts course, meeting twice weekly, for the duration of the term. Students are also invited to "drop in" to the lab during any free period.

Students first review basic computer skills in order to function competently and enjoyably in the lab. They begin their music technology journey by learning keyboard orientation (e.g., how to find middle C). This is followed by discussions and assignments centered on the relationship between intervals and the construction of simple chord progressions in the key of C major.

After the recording and basic keyboard skills are learned and reinforced, students learn to compose and orchestrate pieces with attention to more advanced music and technical skills such as:

♦ Quantizing

♦ Panning

♦ Dynamics

♦ Timbre

♦ Creating drum tracks

♦ Importing and exporting music tracks

♦ Digital and audio recording

The software used at GCDS is user-friendly and offers students a "no-risk" environment for composition and music theory work. Editing is not difficult and children are comfortable and successful using these programs.

Music Software Used at GCDS

Musicshop   32-Track sequencing and notation pro-
                   gram
                   Prints parts
                   Imports and exports standard MIDI files
                   Easy to view
                   Level: Beginners

Free Style   State-of-the-art sequencing and notation
                   Features multiple "take" recording
                   Easy to use editing features
                   Select drum grooves instead of metro-
                   nome click
                   Level: Grades 7–9

Band-In-A-Box   An automatic MIDI accompaniment pro-
                   gram
                   Program instantly generates an accompa-
                   niment in the style of your choice
                   Export standard MIDI files to any other
                   software program
                   Level: Grades 5 and up

Finale   Powerful notation software
                   Choose from 30 templates
                   Seven different ways to enter music
                   New online documentation
                   Hyperscribe, enter music in real-time
                   Comprehensive tool palettes
                   Level: Advanced students; grades 7–9

SPECIAL OUTCOMES, RESULTS, AND ACCOMPLISHMENTS

Music Technology at GCDS is a program that enhances
and enriches traditional music programs such as band, cho-
rus, and general music, as well as adding depth to the curriculum. Specific outcomes include:

   ♦ Music Technology students entered, and won, a
     contest sponsored by The American Cancer Socie-
     ty's Great American Smokeout campaign. They

composed and recorded a digital soundtrack for a
radio commercial, using the skills learned in the
school's music technology lab. This public service
announcement was aired on Connecticut radio
stations during the month of November 1996

◆ As a result of their music technology skills, students can now create MIDI files to use in their
academic multimedia presentations. This adds an
exciting dimension to a child's science or history
report

◆ Students can download (and upload) standard
MIDI files from the Internet

◆ Music Technology attracts a new population of
students to the music department: students who
are not necessarily performers, but who are interested in computers, electronic keyboards, and the
technological aspects of the program

DIFFICULTIES (ANTICIPATED AND UNANTICIPATED)

◆ *Time commitment:* Learning new computer software can be very time-consuming. Music teachers need to be aware of this commitment before
launching new technology programs

◆ *Training:* Getting started can be a daunting experience for the nontechie. There are many challenges
in designing a lab, getting trained, choosing the
instruments, computers, and music software. The
good news is that help is available. For help with
lab design, instruments, training, and computers,
contact:

> SoundTree
> 316 South Service Road
> Melville, NY 11747-3201
> (800) 963-TREE; (516)393-8535
> SoundTree@korgusa.com
> http://www.triplesoft.com/SoundTree

THINGS TO CONSIDER

- ♦ Music Technology needs to be taught by a trained musician who will bring to the subject a body of knowledge and a lifetime of experience
- ♦ Troubleshooting: All of the hardware and software companies offer tech support to their customers

COSTS

Six workstations: $25,000
                   6 Korg X3 Instruments
                   6 Macintosh computers
                   1 GEC (Group Educational Controller)
Software: $3,500
Training: $3,000

CONTACT INFORMATION

Debra A. Lewis, Chair
The Department of Performing and Visual Arts
(203) 622-8517
e-mail: jlpq@aol.com

HORIZON'S TECHNOLOGY VANGUARD TEAM

GOALS OF TECHNOLOGY PROGRAM

♦ To increase student achievement through technology

♦ To train teachers on effective use of technology in the classroom

KEYWORDS

♦ Staff development

♦ Technology training

LOCATION

Horizon Community Middle School
3981 S. Reservoir Rd.
Aurora, CO 80013

DESCRIPTION OF SCHOOL AND COMMUNITY

♦ Grades 6–8

♦ Approximately 1,500 students with 125 faculty members

♦ The school facility is approximately 15 years old

♦ 20% of the school's students are minorities; 15% of students qualify for free or reduced lunches. The halls are brimming with a population that has diverse needs, varying abilities, eclectic interests, and multiethnic backgrounds, all of which drive Horizon's programs

♦ The school's faculty members are focused on learning, are dedicated to meeting the needs of a changing student population in whatever manner is necessary, and willing to take risks to accomplish that task

DESCRIPTION OF PROGRAM

Technology plays a significant role in the delivery of information at Horizon Middle School. In order to put these tools in the hands of students, Horizon believes it is critical to provide staff development to teachers.

The Cherry Creek School District has supported its technology investment by providing a Student Achievement Specialist (SAS) at each school. Realizing that effective staff development must be site-based, planned, and ongoing, the SAS helps school personnel fuse technology and curriculum, thereby enhancing student achievement.

Horizon has made a significant impact with regard to the implementation of technology. Under the leadership of the SAS, a Technology Vanguard team comprised of 12 teachers from different grade levels and curricular areas was created. This team of teachers made a commitment to work together twice a month receiving training and working on classroom technology integration. Providing training for these teachers was crucial to their success in the classroom. Allotting time to work on the equipment and to discuss ties to curriculum was valuable to them. As they increased their personal skills and looked at ways to use technology as a tool in their classrooms, a cluster of five computers was provided for each Vanguard teacher to support their integration of technology.

Watching the growth of the Vanguard teachers and the students in their classrooms created an environment that other staff members noticed. Staff members began asking to be a part of the Vanguard team. Enthusiasm and excitement for computers spread fast. Classes had to be held after school to meet the increasing demand. The SAS had to reevaluate the program in order to continue to train Vanguard leaders and to begin addressing the needs of new Vanguard members. Because of the commitment to training teachers, Horizon students are reaping the benefits of this program.

Types and Examples of Technology Training

October	Computer basics and networks; gradebook
November	Content area software exploration; ClarisWorks
December	Slide shows via ClarisWorks and Kid Pix; giant graphics
January	HyperStudio (1 full day)
February	Multimedia with Apple Computers (2 full days)
March	Multimedia in-house
April	Web pages; curriculum integration
May	Video in the classroom; celebration

SPECIAL OUTCOMES, RESULTS, AND ACCOMPLISHMENTS

To move to an environment that is more student-centered requires support for the teacher and a certain element of risk as they move to a more facilitative role. Assisted by the Student Achievement Specialist, teachers can seek the help and support they need while implementing their lesson plans. Creating model classrooms that incorporate technology as a tool for learning has stimulated both the Vanguard teachers and other faculty members.

Looking toward the future, the school's aim is to encourage this group of Vanguard teachers to train other faculty members and to continue the movement to put technology into the hands of students.

DIFFICULTIES (ANTICIPATED AND UNANTICIPATED)

Areas of difficulty primarily centered on the issue of time. It is the biggest obstacle. Looking at alternative ways to provide staff development was a constant focus.

Additional difficulties centered on having adequate hardware in the classroom to complete desired tasks.

THINGS TO CONSIDER

- ◆ Write grants for release time
- ◆ Apply to receive credit for training time
- ◆ Look outside the box in terms of finding time

COSTS

Most of the equipment needed was already available in-house, but was not being used effectively. Through the district's technology plan, the school purchased the Multimedia Learning Tools Bundle from Apple Computers that consisted of software, hardware (5 Power Macs), and staff development for 12 teachers ($16,000). The Multimedia Learning Tools Bundle provided a critical mass of computers that could be moved into a teacher's classroom.

In addition, $4,500 was used for substitute time for 12 teachers to participate in three full-day training sessions and to cover copying costs.

CONTACT INFORMATION

Christine Archer-Davison
Teaching, Learning, and Technology Specialist
Student Achievement Resource Center
Office of Technology
14188 E. Briarwood Avenue
Englewood, CO 80112
(303) 486-4003
e-mail: cdavison@ccsd.k12.co.us

HYPER AND HOT: A NEW LOOK AT THE RESEARCH PAPER

GOALS OF TECHNOLOGY PROGRAM

- To encourage students to plan software products that are informative, easy-to-use, and attractive
- To increase students' computer skills
- To promote critical thinking and problem solving skills
- To introduce students to graphic design

KEYWORDS

- Authoring
- Cooperative learning
- Multimedia

LOCATION

Seminole High School
2701 Ridgewood Avenue
Sanford, FL 32773

DESCRIPTION OF SCHOOL AND COMMUNITY

- Grades 9–12
- Approximately 2,100 students and 120 teachers
- The school is approximately 35 years old
- Sanford is located on the shores of Lake Monroe and the St. Johns River. Sanford is the home of many things that would draw people to the area, including the Central Florida Zoo, the Marina, a large modern shopping mall, and a renovated downtown shopping area with many antique stores. More than 36,000 year-round residents call

Sanford home, and approximately 1,500 are winter residents. The school's population is 57.6%
Caucasian, 35% African American, 1.9% Asian,
5% Hispanic, and 0.4% American Indian. Seminole High School, Seminole County's oldest high
school, has an Academy of Health Careers magnet program and is in the process of implementing a second magnet program, the International
Baccalaureate

DESCRIPTION OF PROGRAM

In an attempt to make the traditional, typed technical research report more relevant to tomorrow's workplace, an
English teacher assigned her students the task of creating
computer programs that presented their research in an interactive format. Cooperative groups had to agree on a topic
that related to the science or mathematics they were studying, plan their research strategies, and design the format,
structure, and flow of the pieces or components of their computer applications. In a miniworkshop, the media specialist
demonstrated and explained the use of Authority, an authoring software program that the school already owned, and
students practiced the basics of creating screens, text, graphics, and "buttons" that, when activated, would take the user
to new information. Work took place in an existing computer
lab with Tandy 386 computers.

Many students had never used a computer or a mouse;
none of the students had ever designed an interactive program. Preliminary work consisted of a combination of media
center research for information on their topics and plans for
presentation of this information. Using a teacher-designed
storyboard template, groups planned their layouts and as
many details as possible before entering the computer lab. In
the lab, each student worked on his or her own section or
"module," saving it on a disk so it could be later added to the
group's master report.

Original graphics were designed with a paint program
within the Authority software, and scanned pictures were
imported. An ongoing process of editing and revision culmi-

nated in class presentations and peer evaluations of the finished products. Run-time disks that could be loaded as programs on any computer were created for distribution. The scope of this project necessitated the use of alternative assessment methods. Rather than lending itself to the "red pen treatment," the project developed students' ability and desire to evaluate their own work. While the instructors monitored and observed the process on a daily basis, the real evaluation came when the students presented their programs to each other. The true criteria for assessment were the ease of use of the product, the relevance and accuracy of the information presented, the appearance of the screens, the "interactiveness" of the program, and the reactions of peers. Class members provided oral and written feedback as each program was presented.

SPECIAL OUTCOMES, RESULTS, AND ACCOMPLISHMENTS

English teachers have traditionally taught research paper writing as a linear process: outline, note cards, rough draft, editing, and final draft. This project took a more spatial approach, using flowcharts, graphics, continual revision, and group conferencing and consensus. Instead of dry research and reporting, students took a problem and solved it, using all their critical thinking and group skills. Students found that they had to abandon what didn't work, polish their successes, and continue the process until they had accomplished their goals. The end result was active instead of passive and had to be user-friendly, requiring the creators to intuit the needs of the consumer/user.

Every project was unique, reflecting the diversity of learning styles and the creativity of the designers. Teachers became facilitators of learning rather than authoritarian instructors. Clarity of communication and correct grammar, often taught as desired outcomes of writing assignments, were means rather than ends: tools with which students relayed information, integrating their fields of study in a new way.

DIFFICULTIES (ANTICIPATED AND UNANTICIPATED)

The authoring software package that was used, Authority, runs slowly on a 386 machine. Students who were used to 486s and Pentiums found themselves impatient with the execution time of program commands. However, the older computer lab was the only place on campus where most members of a class could have access to individual computers. Another difficulty was that the software program uses only PCX format graphics. Also, the program allows for the addition of sound, but without sound cards in the machines adding sound was impossible. It is clear that to fully utilize this program, as well HyperStudio, which was purchased, an investment in new multimedia computers is necessary.

COSTS

An existing computer lab was utilized. The only cost was the cost of the authoring software and the flatbed color scanner that was used for graphics. Any authoring software package, such as HyperStudio, would have allowed the program to accomplish its objectives, but Authority would run on the machines that were available. The Authority package price for a single user is $99 and a 25-station network license is $1,800. The price for the HP Scanjet 4c color scanner was approximately $900.

CONTACT INFORMATION

Lynn Cullum
Media Specialist
(407) 320-5028
(407) 320-5024 (Fax)
e-mail: Lynn_Cullum@scps.k12.fl.us

Jane Cooper
English Teacher
(407) 320-5050
(407) 320-5024 (Fax)
e-mail: Jane_Cooper@scps.k12.fl.us

HYPERMOTIVATING THROUGH SOCIAL STUDIES

GOALS OF TECHNOLOGY PROGRAM

- To bring traditional studies to life through use of technology
- To integrate technology effectively into middle school social studies courses
- To help students learn to use technologies to enhance learning

KEYWORDS

- Curriculum integration
- Laptop computers
- Multimedia
- Social studies
- Telecommunications

LOCATION

Worcester Country School
PO Box 1006
508 S. Main Street
Berlin, MD 21811

DESCRIPTION OF SCHOOL AND COMMUNITY

- Grades preschool–12
- Approximately 460 students and 50 teachers

♦ Worcester Country School is an independent college preparatory school in a rural/resort community. Students come from a four-county, two-state area on the Delmarva Peninsula.

DESCRIPTION OF PROGRAM

At Worcester Country School, faculty members were anxious to integrate technology effectively into the curriculum. To do this, middle school students (grades 6–8) were scheduled to be in the computer labs for social studies periods. Sixth graders use the Lower School lab for social studies classes each day and have an additional computer instruction period weekly. Students in Grades 7 and 8 have three scheduled periods in the Upper School lab for social studies and two additional periods for computer instruction. eMate portable computers are available for use in Grades 7 and 8 social studies. In their regular classrooms, students use these small computers for note taking, outlining, and graphic organizations of their studies. Teachers have found them extremely useful and durable and were surprised by the battery life (about 25 hours) and the speed with which the batteries recharge. "I love using them and so do my students," says teacher Connie Lampkin. "You can put them in any classroom without having to add more electrical outlets. The students especially enjoy 'beaming' ideas to others when working on group projects. This technology has added both flexibility and excitement to our program."

Besides use of the eMates and class time in the computer labs, students can be found in the labs before and after school as they continue their work. "They want to stay," explains Lampkin, "for they are eager to create the best projects possible." Many also take their work home on disks to perfect the work on family computers. Parents often ask what programs are being used at school so that they can have them at home. According to one parent, "It's so good to see my child eager to refine his school work; he is so interested in social studies this year."

Traditional social studies content is covered in the courses: Grade 6, Ancient History; Grade 7, American History; and Grade 8, World Geography. These courses differ from other courses in the amount of time the students spend using technology and the teaching methods, not in content. There are no textbooks for Grade 6, but Grades 7 and 8 students use American history and geography texts. Originally, there was a textbook in Grade 6, but the teacher, after teaching the course for several years, suggested that the textbook was not needed. Her feeling was that the material for the course could be obtained through traditional and online resources, along with her notes and guidance. Because 1997–98 was the first year of doing the program in Grades 7 and 8, it was decided that it would be best to retain the textbooks, at least for this year.

At the beginning of the school year, students learn to use graphic organizers that are created on their computers. These organizers help the students to work effectively with information, to learn the needed content, and to prepare for reports and presentations. Guidelines are established with each class and with parents regarding the standards for research, grading, and reports. The classroom teacher and the computer teacher work together to insure that the needed software is on the target computers and that Internet connections are functioning. They also help students learn what is expected of them. Students new to the program, such as sixth grade students and new students in Grades 7 and 8, need a bit more help, but they catch on quickly. Besides the graphic organizers, student projects might include creating historical newspapers; making cartoons and animations; developing slide shows; publishing reports; finding and organizing information from the school library and the Internet; and creating interactive presentations. Except when the teacher is giving a whole group lesson, she is working with groups or individuals. The students, involved in their studies, do not notice visitors watching them, but the visitors notice how these students are helping each other and discussing the content on their own. The students are taking a leadership role in their learning. The teacher has set the guidelines and standards that allow the students to take off on their learning experiences.

Among the software used are these programs: Microsoft Works, eMate word processing and graphics, Digital Chisel,

Kid Pix Studio, HyperStudio, ClarisWorks, Encarta Encyclopedia, Ancient Lands, Encyclopedia Britannica online, map and atlas programs, and Web browsers. Site links from Apple's Curricular Theme (http://ed.info.apple.com/education/techlearn/ccenter/curriccenter.html) have been very useful to Grade 7 students in particular. Other software programs put to use, as needed, are digital and video cameras.

SPECIAL OUTCOMES, RESULTS, AND ACCOMPLISHMENTS

Integrating technology into traditional course studies not only provides motivation for learning, it helps students use the content and remember what they have studied. Social studies, taught in the computer labs, is a favorite subject among students. Students in these classes love to talk about the subject matter and how they are using computers and telecommunications in their studies. They are proud of their work and it shows! Throughout the courses, these students are practicing their writing, research, editing, critical thinking, and presentation skills.

The course teachers and the computer specialists work together as a team. They've developed wonderful ideas for the course, as have their students who are also part of the team.

DIFFICULTIES (ANTICIPATED AND UNANTICIPATED)

These courses do not require a technology specialist; they do require a good classroom teacher who is willing to learn how to use technology with students. The teacher must be flexible enough to try new methods of teaching and to help students and parents adjust to these methods. Bright, enthusiastic teachers who love to do projects with students are excellent candidates for these courses. The teachers have to be willing to troubleshoot when problems arise and to spend time with students beyond the school day. Many students will ask to continue their work after school because they "just have to add some special parts to projects."

Students must have time in the school schedule to access computers for these courses. Originally, because of lack of time in the computer labs, the Grade 6 course was done for a half-year. There were numerous complaints from students and parents when students returned to the classrooms for social studies. One student's comment was, "What do I have to do to bribe you into letting me stay in the lab for social studies?" Another offered this solution: "I think we could stay here and serve as tutors for the other section, and we could do presentations by sharing the computers."

The teacher must keep after some students to add text to presentations and reports. Some students will do graphics, animation, sound, and so forth throughout if requirements for text input are not set.

Because the teachers enjoy this method of teaching so much, they want to have all their classes in the labs. Other teachers are interested, too, but there simply isn't enough time.

THINGS TO CONSIDER

Although these courses provide an excellent way to fully integrate technology into one area of the curriculum, parents and school administrators have to be convinced that such courses are worthwhile. Parents and school administrators want students to learn to use technology effectively, but they do not want students to miss getting the content. Preparing parents and administrators for this way of teaching through a gentle, but effective public relations effort is important.

COSTS

Schools would need enough computers (multimedia capable with CD-ROM drives, adequate memory, and Internet connections) for a class to use either in a lab environment or through laptop technology. Presentation , word processing, database with graphics options, paint, CD-ROM encyclopedias and atlases, software that goes with the course work (optional), and telecommunications software are needed. The school has found it best to use a television connected to the teacher's computer for display, because the LCD projection is difficult to see.

Because these are regular school courses, there are no additional expenses. The equipment and much of the software is used for other classes in the school.

CONTACT INFORMATION

Dr. Merle Marsh
Head of the Lower School
410-641-3575
410-641-3586 (Fax)
e-mail: marsh@shore.intercom.net or merlem@aol.com

IGNITING THE PIONEER SPIRIT

GOALS OF TECHNOLOGY PROGRAM

♦ To develop an Internet site for the school that uniquely serves the larger community and that can be used as a global resource

♦ To build meaningful connections between history, geography, technology, daily living, and community relations

♦ To build awareness of global relations and communications, encouraging students to view themselves as ambassadors

KEYWORDS

♦ History

♦ Internet

♦ Multimedia

♦ Natural resources

♦ Video

LOCATION

Alta Elementary School
21771 E. Parlier Avenue
Reedley, CA 93654

DESCRIPTION OF SCHOOL AND COMMUNITY

♦ Grades K–6

♦ Approximately 425 students and 22 teachers

♦ Facility was built in 1955

♦ Alta Elementary School is in Kings Canyon Unified School District at the center of California's

San Joaquin Valley. Alta is proud of its ethnic diversity. The student body is composed of Filipino, Hispanic, American Indian, Asian American, African American, and Caucasian students. Alta has received numerous awards for its innovative programs and the academic achievements of its students.

DESCRIPTION OF PROGRAM

This project has been evolving since 1994 as students have explored telecommunications and developed original Internet projects. Alta Elementary School has been weaving a tapestry of history, heritage, and legends that reflects its community. They are adding stories of the earth and of how crops are nurtured and grown. From the land comes the most fundamental of human relationships and exchanges—the food and bread we eat—a foundation that all technologies rely on.

The Reedley area is rich in agricultural and natural resources and has been known as the World's Fruit Basket since 1946. It is also referred to as the gateway to Sequoia/Kings Canyon National Park. Kings River flows through the community and has the distinction of being only second to the Nile River in the amount of farmland it irrigates. Alta's site and local community encompasses historical landmarks (manmade and natural), and historical contributions of individuals that are related to these sites (famous and otherwise) in the Reedley area. Individuals from all over the world have settled in this beautiful agricultural area. The school's collection of stories, articles, and photos creates a scenic portrait of historic Reedley, the fragrant and fruitful Blossom Trail, and the majestic Sierras nearby.

The school's Web site contains a related collection of stories, articles, photos, and memorabilia that offers glimpses into Reedley's past and present charm. Sites of historic relevance are shown, and areas of historic significance are described. Students have shared pioneer stories of family members, keypals, and founding fathers of Reedley. Members of the Reedley Chamber of Commerce and Historical Society have contributed information. Modern-day pioneers have shared stories as well and created a truly global portrait.

Each year the project grows in originality from the beginning theme. The rapid changes in technology continue to make the pioneer topic popular and relevant to new groups of students. Alta began a historical anthology theme with a nationwide project that formally launched January 5, 1998, called "Patty Reed's Doll." New stories and adventures unfold as two travel buddies trek across the United States collecting tales of westward travel. The two final destinations are Sutter's Fort in Sacramento, and the Willamette Valley in Oregon. The project ended in June 1998 and videos are to be distributed to participants in the fall. Plans are underway for another anthology (on a worldwide theme) to begin in August 1998.

There are many lesson plans, samples of student work, and other relevant information on the site. These are posted in the hope that other teachers will find them useful and inspiring, and use them to help students develop their own original historical sites. The only request the school makes is that people provide feedback on the information they use and provide links to the work that they develop, so the tapestry can grow in its depth, scope, and impact.

A sample of student work and one lesson plan are included here to give an idea of materials that are posted. The philosophy is that every teacher's classroom contains a unique combination of personalities, abilities, learning and teaching styles. For this reason, ideas are kept flexible and creative to allow teachers to develop lessons and activities that they and their students can feel ownership for and that can become their own unique accomplishments. Many ideas are suitable for any grade level or range of ability. Much of this has been done with students who have learning disabilities. This assignment could easily be modified or made more complex for more advanced students. Suggestions for doing so are often included.

Exploring the Family Tree

Each student is given about two weeks for the following assignment:

> We have been learning about pioneers and explorers. Ask your family (parents, grandparents,

aunts or uncles) about your family history. Where did your ancestors (parents, grandparents, great-grandparents) come from? How were they like explorers or pioneers? Find at least one interesting TRUE story about your family history to share with the class.

Write down this information. (This next part could be deleted where appropriate.) Your parents can help or do the writing for you. You do the interviewing.

After the teacher receives this, the students are asked to do more writing with the information they gathered. How is this information meaningful to them? How does it make them feel to learn these things about their family? What new ventures might they decide to pursue now or in the future?

From this lesson, and the activities that followed, came the following two letters. The first letter arrived weeks before the 50-year remembrance of the Holocaust (an event the students were completely unaware of beforehand). It eloquently expresses the power the Internet has. The second letter was written entirely by special education students. They spent two days writing it and agonized, deliberated, and discussed many choices of words to find the vocabulary to express their emotions.

Dear Mandy,

I guess I am one of those not-so-famous pioneers. I actually have been a pioneer in more than one way. I am a child of a survivor of the Holocaust. I have long believed it is my duty to get the message out what one man can do to another. My father is still alive; however, he is the sole survivor of his family. There were a total of 144 family members; all died in WW II.

I came to the United States on April 28, 1959. I was 8 years old. My father came here for the rich opportunities this country provided. He was not able to obtain a proper education during his teens because he was imprisoned. His opportunities in our homeland were limited. Our country was also severely overpopulated. The government had encouraged families to have more children, and stipends were offered. Well, that backfired. There wasn't enough housing for all these people. Quite often a married couple had to wait six years to get an apartment of their own. This meant they lived with their parents during this time. Houses were not very large in Amsterdam. To relieve this problem, the government paid people to emigrate. My dad took them up on it.

We were sponsored by a professional soccer team in San Francisco. He had friends who already lived here. When we landed in New York, we did not go through Ellis Island, but we might as well have. We were sequestered in a booth. We were frightened. No one to talk to. We were questioned. I don't know about what since I did not speak English. We were late for our plane. We even had to switch airports in New York. When we got to the ticket counter my dad was told he owed more money. He had $100 in his pocket. He had to pay $40 extra. We found out we were going on a jet. I was scared. The only jets I had seen before were jet fighters. When we arrived in San Francisco the news media was there in full force photographing everyone on the plane. We received a certificate, which I could not read. It said we were aviation pioneers. We flew on the first transcontinental flight on a passenger jet.

Because we traveled on the jet, the people who were supposed to pick us up were not there. We arrived nearly a day ahead of time. My dad did not know how to use the phone. His English was limited. It took a long time, but he finally connected. We had to wait a long time since they lived an hour away from the airport and they had to finish work.

All this in one day. Hope you find this interesting. It is as clear in my mind as the day I lived it. Please write again.

Sophia Smith

Dear Mrs. Smith,

I have asked my class to write a collaborative letter to you, because your story reflects so much of what we are learning through our Pioneer Project. The story made us feel sad, because your family was killed during WW II. People should be more intelligent, conscientious, and compassionate toward each other. Maybe we can help people gather together, to be kind to each other. Unfortunately, we see fighting, driveby shootings, robbery, drugs, drinking too much, senseless deaths. How can we help make a difference? We are growing up in a violent world. Pioneers showed how they survived, endured, had courage, were brave when it wasn't easy, were noble, and built a better world and community. Your father is a hero and shows all of these qualities. By studying about other pioneers, we hope to become stronger, be willing to work harder so we can make the world safer, be accepting of other cultures. This is so important for the world.

How many were in your family when you came to the United States? Do you remember somebody being nice and kind on the day you came to America? What was it like when you went to school? Were there any children who spoke Dutch? How was life different in America from Holland?

One student's grandfather was a helicopter pilot in WW II. He was killed in action. Another student's family was in a concentration camp in California. His family lost all their property. It is really terrible how shameful people can sometimes act.

Maybe communicating through projects like this on the Internet can help people become more passionate about life and its value and meaning. People need to be more caring, trustworthy, and treat people the way they would like to be treated. When you see your father at spring break, tell him Mrs. Vitali's class wishes him the very best. We will try to be individuals willing to make the world a better place and take a stand for what is right.

With deepest feelings,

Mrs. Vitali's Class

The project becomes more intriguing as other schools and students do their own explorations into their unique historical roots.

This continually growing work becomes increasingly complex as other communities and schools around the world are contribute to this project. The agrarian and pioneer lifestyles reflect qualities showing the tremendous strength and potential of the human spirit to endure and even to prosper despite tremendous adversity. In a rapidly changing world, there are treasures and lessons to be found and preserved for future generations.

SPECIAL OUTCOMES, RESULTS, AND ACCOMPLISHMENTS

- ♦ Alta has become recognized as a model in technology integration into the curriculum
- ♦ Students have learned to present information to a global audience and have hosted international guests and visitors
- ♦ Students are learning a wide variety of technical skills
- ♦ Strong partnerships between school, businesses, and community have been formed including partnerships with Kings Canyon Educational Partnership Foundation; Fresno County Office of

Education; California State University, Fresno; Fresno Pacific University; Reedley Historical Society; Reedley Chamber of Commerce; Mobynet; Global School Net; California Telemation Project; Videonics; and Iomega

DIFFICULTIES (ANTICIPATED AND UNANTICIPATED)

Time management is probably the greatest difficulty. This project has grown tremendously, but no formal funding of actual services supports it. It relies on volunteer efforts and commitments of students, teachers, and parents. The lack of a formal computer lab makes it difficult for many students to work simultaneously on project additions. New equipment has been funded through mentor funds, minigrants, and direct donations from hardware/software companies.

COSTS

Internet connections: $144/year
            (The program is awaiting schoolwide connections. Thus far, this work has been done with one school connection and dedicated line using $25,000 in state funds to provide connectivity.)
Phone line: $300/year
Training: No cost
            (Collaborations with California State University, Fresno and Fresno County Office of Education have provided numerous facilities and opportunities for training. Students work at recesses and after school. Teachers have also received informal training during in-service days.)
Server Space: No cost
            (Server space donated by Global School Net, Fresno Pacific University, and Mobynet)
Iomega Zip drives: $250
Power PC with AV capabilities: $2,300
Apple 150 Quick take camera, Hitachi camcorder, Videonics TitleMaker 3000, Radio Shack mixer,

two Hitachi VCRs (one SVSH) and 13-inch
televisions for editing station with an Aiwa
sound system for editing (grants and spon-
sorships reduced costs by $1,500): $3,250

CONTACT INFORMATION

Cheryl Vitali
Resource Specialist/District Technology Mentor
(209) 637-1268
(209) 637-1298 (Fax)
e-mail: cvitali@telis.org
http://cyberfair.gsn.org/altakcusd/hhll.html

INTEGRATING MULTIPLE
TECHNOLOGIES AND DISCIPLINES:
FAB's wRIGHT PLACE
AMUSEMENT PARK

GOALS OF TECHNOLOGY PROGRAM

- ◆ To develop facility with and awareness of a range of technology skills and applications
- ◆ To effectively integrate all content areas with visual and performing arts
- ◆ To provide a child-centered learning environment with numerous opportunities for hands-on, realistic application of content, skills, and tools
- ◆ To foster awareness of the pervasive nature of technology in a wide range of careers
- ◆ To motivate interest in science and technology

KEYWORDS

- ◆ Curriculum integration
- ◆ Internet
- ◆ Multimedia
- ◆ SCANS competencies

LOCATION

Fogelsville Elementary School
312 S. Route 100
Allentown, PA 18106

DESCRIPTION OF SCHOOL AND COMMUNITY

- ◆ Grades K–6
- ◆ Approximately 620 students and 60 staff members

♦ Fogelsville Elementary School is located on 12 acres of rolling farmland in the Parkland School District. The school, designed to reflect the heritage of its Lehigh County location, has been enlarged twice since its 1965 opening. Farmland on one side contrasts with extensive growth on the other sides of warehouses, warehouse distribution centers, and office buildings

DESCRIPTION OF PROGRAM

FAB's wRIGHT PLACE Amusement Park is an interdisciplinary project suited to upper elementary and secondary students. Initially seeded by a National Science Teachers Association/Toyota Tapestry grant, the program provided opportunities for students to explore multiple technologies through the design and building of a working model amusement park. Students selected and utilized appropriate technological tools to accomplish their goals. Hammer and nails, cutting tools, multimedia references, multimedia authoring programs, visual diagramming software, desktop publishing, flatbed scanners, cameras, the Internet, and scientific equipment provided FAB (Fogelsville Architects & Builders) fifth graders with an impressive array of research and construction tools.

Successful implementation of this project required development of a sense of teamwork. To initiate this project teamwork, the group began by investigating the use of symbols to convey information. Students then worked together to design a logo for their enterprise. T-shirts sporting this logo provided a visual symbol of the team during all special events such as field trips, classroom visits, and performances.

Students then read a *Smithsonian* article about crash dummies and constructed their own model dummies, complete with impact points. This led to the writing of anthropomorphic crash dummy tales. The blend of fact and fiction about their own personal dummies proved to be an inspiring combination for the budding authors. The size of the dummies established the scale of the park rides (1:20).

After experimenting and developing a background in basic physics concepts, students designed and built several park rides. Deciding on the use of endangered or threatened species for the carousel animals prompted considerable electronic research (see figure below). Students utilized multimedia references (Dangerous Creatures, Encarta) in the research process to select the endangered or threatened species included on their Conservation Carousel. Computer-based references and Internet resources provided students with data and illustrations to proceed with the design and creation of the carousel animals. Similar research led to the naming of the Cheetah Coaster (named for the fastest land animal).

The animals on the carousel were chosen through
electronic research for their status as endangered species.
© Fogelsville Elementary School

Students test their Viper Coaster.
© Fogelsville Elementary School

Students read about ladybugs and used the software program Inspiration to create concept maps to organize their information to design The Bumper Bugs ride. The cars for this
ride were built to resemble aphids (dinner for the ladybugs).
Ladybug plastic wands (fly swatters) were outfitted with
magnets, as were the aphid cars. The cars were propelled by
magnetic repulsion. The floor for the bumper car arena was
an overflow pan from a hot water heater. The vertical framework, built from Erector parts, was painted to look like a
trellis.

Students utilized the Internet and multimedia references
as they partnered with another fifth grade class to research
and create timelines. Seven groups of students each took a
20-year period to cover the past 140 years. The top portion of
the timelines covered events related to the history of amusement parks, related rides, and technologies. The bottom portion of the timelines contained events in United States history. This parallel development allowed students to visualize

what the cultural climate was like at the peak of amusement park development.

Students also learned about the history of the railroads, particularly the development of the transcontinental railroad. This knowledge provided the basis for their $18.69 Train Ride, an HO scale model that circled the center of their model park. Imagine the excitement of two trains coming head-to-head on the same track, but stopping at the last moment! Replicas of the original engines, Jupiter and the 119, were provided by Union Pacific for this endeavor. The students experimented with designing train layouts on the computer and created train poems and posters with a first grade class. A clothoid loop coaster, The Viper, and Erector Ferris Wheels rounded out the park rides.

A cardiologist visited the class to share information on healthy eating and exercise habits. The students used this information to create nutritious menus for their park food stands. Each student then built a model stand that matched his or her menu. Food places sported such names as the Eagle's Nest, The Rain Forest Café, FABulous Fruit Snax, and the wRIGHT Foods!

FAB's wRIGHT PLACE takes its name from the architectural inspiration found in the work of Frank Lloyd Wright. Students used information gleaned from The Ultimate Frank Lloyd Wright CD and a lecture by Harvard University expert Dr. Neil Levine to design the clerestory windows for the carousel pavilion and arrange the model park. (See figure on page 153.) The park layout itself was a zone design, patterned after Wright's design of Wingspread. The group discovered via the Internet that Wingspread, also known as Pinwheel House, was undergoing roof repairs and other renovations. The Hillier Group, in charge of these modifications, provided the students with numerous photographs, diagrams, and background information.

Internationally renowned architect Matthew Hoey, also inspired by Frank Lloyd Wright, utilizes modern material in novel ways. He visited the classroom to share his perspective on the design process. His visit was the start of many letter-writing opportunities as the students communicated with their community supporters.

The students created abstract stained windows for the
pavilion after studying the designs of Frank Lloyd Wright.
© Fogelsville Elementary School

Julie, don't you know?, a show written and produced by the
students, extended the learning experience. Content area
concepts, especially physics, combined with rewritten lyrics
to the oldies and an amusement park setting to provide an
avenue for students to present their experiences to the school
and community. A dance instructor from the community
helped the students polish their choreography. This one-hour
show tells the story of Julie, a student who comes to a new
class midyear. She is not happy about joining a class immersed in the study of physics. Sent to the lunchroom to buy
tickets, she discovers that her lunch ticket is actually a ticket
to FAB's wRIGHT PLACE Amusement Park. Isaac Newton
and the park employees, who look suspiciously like her new
schoolmates, teach her about physics as they help her become
one of the group. Scanned images and Microsoft Publisher
were used to create show posters, invitations, and programs.
The students also utilized their show information and scanned images as they explored how to create a HyperStudio
multimedia program.

The culminating activity for the project took place at Dorney Park, a local amusement park. The students had the opportunity to display their scale park in juxtaposition to the real thing. Teams of students took turns explaining their project to the general public while their classmates explored the wonders of full-sized rides.

The FAB program supports active learning as workplace expertise is taught with consideration of the SCANS competencies. This project supports the development of identified foundation skills and workplace competencies. Career awareness was developed as students assumed related project roles and through contact with community professionals.

It is beyond the scope of this publication to thoroughly cover this program in depth. Additional information about the learning environment as it relates to this project can be found under the case study on the PA Link to Learn Web site: http://L2L.org. Information about obtaining the video "The Kids are Wired" can also be accessed at the Web site. Link to Learn has also produced a professional development CD-ROM.

SPECIAL OUTCOMES, RESULTS, AND ACCOMPLISHMENTS

Student work on this project was truly exceptional. Their experiences have been shared in The *Christian Science Monitor* and *Woman's Day* magazine. The video "The Kids are Wired" has been shown on Pennsylvania PBS stations. They are also featured as a case study on the PA Link to Learn Web site and the related professional development CD-ROM.

DIFFICULTIES (ANTICIPATED AND UNANTICIPATED)

The program is material, space, and time intensive. Organization and management skills are crucial. A work center carousel, complete with pegboard carousel animals, was built to organize materials for this project.

THINGS TO CONSIDER

The program could be scaled down to reduce time, material, and space demands. The theme of the park and rides can be altered to reflect a variety of interest areas. In addition, the work of various architects and/or artists could serve as a basis for the park's design.

COSTS

A $7,900 grant from NSTA/Toyota Tapestry seeded the project.

Hardware costs have declined significantly since the inception of this project. Suitable flatbed scanners can be purchased for approximately $99.00. Multimedia computers can be purchased for under $1,000.00. Student construction tools and building materials can be purchased from The Science Source, PO Box 727, Waldoboro, ME 04572 (207-832-7281). *The Journey Inside the Computer,* available to educators at no cost from Intel Corporation, provides students with an understanding of microcomputer systems and networking.

CONTACT INFORMATION

Winnifred G. Bolinsky
Fifth Grade Teacher
(610) 398-0331
e-mail: wbolinsky@msn.com

INTEGRATING TECHNOLOGY INTO THE CURRICULUM

GOALS OF TECHNOLOGY PROGRAM

- To allow each learner to develop skills necessary for a highly technological and changing world
- To make learning more meaningful by integrating technology projects into reading, writing, geography, and science

KEYWORDS

- Internet
- Telecommunications

LOCATION

Waiau Elementary School
98-450 Hookanike Street
Pearl City, HI 96782

DESCRIPTION OF SCHOOL AND COMMUNITY

- Grades K–6
- Approximately 600 students from a middle-class environment
- Approximately 30 teachers
- Facility is approximately 25 years old and is located in the suburbs of Pearl City

DESCRIPTION OF PROGRAM

Technology is integrated throughout the curriculum. For example, projects are presented on the elementary class' Web site (http://www.doe.hawaii.edu/~conniem/).

Students have "keypals" (e-mail penpals), which enables them to use reading, writing, and critical thinking. They learn to ask questions, write sentences, and practice better usage of punctuation and capitalization.

The Newsletter Group provides reading material for the students. They read, discuss, and compare themselves to others. Through geography and mapping, they locate where the newsletter originated. Specific monthly topics make writing considerations easier.

Weather and the SAW (Sky Awareness Week) Project make it possible for students to practice skills such as reading a thermometer and gathering wind and cloud information. Because this information is shared with other schools, they can compare and contrast information.

The latest class project, The Apple Poetry Project, became an extension of an Apple Unit. The students published on a Web page and shared their writings with a larger audience. Incorporated into this unit was the study of the poetry form and the study of geography including what types of apples are grown in different areas. The class posted to a listserv to find out more about apples from other information sources.

SPECIAL OUTCOMES, RESULTS, AND ACCOMPLISHMENTS

The students learned that there is more to the world than their four walls. They learned to use a map and about different places, sharing their reading and writing with other students.

For the teacher, being connected with others outside the teacher's own school and community increases the teacher's awareness and knowledge of others and of what they do at their school or classroom. The teacher becomes part of a larger community of learners—the world.

DIFFICULTIES (ANTICIPATED AND UNANTICIPATED)

Students come to school with a wide range of abilities. Some students have good reading and writing skills, while others are still learning to read and write. As teachers work with the students and their communication skills, instruction can become individualized.

Technology-oriented projects can be time-consuming depending on whether there is a specific topic of study at the teacher's particular grade level.

THINGS TO CONSIDER

Educators need to be open in their thinking and views of curriculum. They must examine how the views of others can add to their teaching and learning. Technology can be easily integrated into the curriculum if educators are flexible. Electronic communications and listservs can facilitate thought and curriculum expansion.

COSTS

There should be Internet connections at home and at school. Home connections provide time for teachers to explore the Internet for telecommunications projects that can be integrated into curriculum. School connections enable the teacher to carry out technology-integrated plans with other subjects and provide a basis for the teacher to show the students actual projects and information online.

CONTACT INFORMATION

Connie Mark
Elementary Teacher
(808) 453-6530
(808) 453-6541 (Fax)
e-mail: conniem@kalama.doe.hawaii.edu
http://www.doe.hawaii.edu/~conniem/

Making a Home
on the Web

Goals of Technology Program

- To design and display original school projects and programs
- To help upper-elementary students make subject area connections to meet instructional standards by using telecommunications technology

Keywords

- Interdisciplinary learning
- Internet
- Telecommunications

Location

Christiansburg Elementary School
Wades Lane and Betty Drive
Christiansburg, VA 24073

Description of School and Community

- Grades 3–5
- Approximately 361 students and 18 teachers
- Facility is approximately 40 years old.
- Christiansburg Elementary School is located in the town of Christiansburg, Virginia, a rural community nestled between the Blue Ridge and Appalachian Mountains. Approximately 42% of its student population is economically disadvantaged; 20% is handicapped; 6% is minorities; and 10% is identified as gifted and talented.

DESCRIPTION OF PROGRAM

The "Web Weavers: Teaching Fifth Graders to Make a Home on the Web" program uses telecommunications technology to create school World Wide Web (WWW) pages. It consists of training a group of fifth graders (Web Weavers) to apply technologies to strategies for problem-solving and critical thinking; select and use technology (computers, computer software, Internet, digital camera, scanner) to design and maintain pages; and create and link Web pages.

Web Weavers begin by learning how to use the Internet as a database for information. By designing their personal home pages, they become proficient at using the computer and Internet connections (Netscape Web browser, File Transfer Protocol), computer software (WordPerfect, HTML Writer, PowerPoint programs), digital camera and scanner operation, and word processing skills. Students also learn how to search and retrieve Internet information from the WWW. For example, they found more than 75 locations for their project TechnoZoo. Working in teams of four, they learn how to lay out pages; they then use images from graphics programs, camera, scanner, and other Internet sources to enhance these pages. They also incorporate WWW searches and other library media in projects. They link projects to the Web pages and transfer those pages to a file box.

By creating Web pages, Web Weavers help support the school and community. The Web Weavers gather and process student products, teacher resources, and other school information. This is how Web Weavers are making a home on the Web. You'll find this award-winning program, along with ideas for creating your own Web pages, on the Christiansburg Elementary School home page (http://www.bev.net/education/schools/ces/).

SPECIAL OUTCOMES, RESULTS, AND ACCOMPLISHMENTS

- Source of information for students, their parents, teachers, and the greater Christiansburg community

- Source of quality, no cost projects and programs

- Exemplary use of educational technology as a learning tool with elementary students

- Training in telecomputing that facilitates life-long learning

- Recognition at the local (Montgomery County Public School), state (Virginia Society for Technology in Education), and national levels (a 1996 winner of the National Student Technology Leadership Competition at the National Educational Computing Conference and awarded 1997 Best School Site)

DIFFICULTIES (ANTICIPATED AND UNANTICIPATED)

Web Weaver students have the opportunity to use sophisticated equipment including a scanner, digital camera, and computer. With this equipment also come problems. For example, the available scanner would only accommodate photo-size pictures, not the larger size drawings needed for the "Art Gallery." The digital camera needs to be recharged frequently. Occasionally, the high-speed Internet connection is inoperable. This provides the students and their teacher-advisors with problem-solving situations.

THINGS TO CONSIDER

- Purchase a computer that easily connects to the Internet

- Avoid expensive and unnecessary purchases of software with Internet userware

- Purchase a scanner and digital camera that meets your needs

◆ Choose students who are bright, independent, and motivated workers

◆ Plan to invest afterschool hours training students and volunteers

COSTS

Hardware:	$2,000 per computer
Digital camera and scanner:	$1,000
Software:	$500

CONTACT INFORMATION

Catherine Ney
(540) 382-5172
(540) 381-6143 (Fax)
e-mail: cney@pen.k12.va.us

NEW TECHNOLOGY HIGH SCHOOL

GOALS OF TECHNOLOGY PROGRAM

- To develop quality, project-based, academically integrated, technology-rich curriculum taught in a professional environment that ensures the education mission of the school
- To prepare students for postsecondary education by completing one semester of college-level work as a high school graduation requirement
- To have students gain skills, experience, and knowledge allowing immediate entrance to high-paying, high-skilled jobs in technology related fields

KEYWORDS

- Curriculum Integration
- Distance learning
- Multimedia
- Project-based learning
- School to Career
- Tech prep

LOCATION

New Technology High School
Napa County
920 Yount Street
Napa, CA 94558

DESCRIPTION OF SCHOOL AND COMMUNITY

- Grades 11–12

- Approximately 220 students and 10 teachers
- Renovated facility is two years old
- New Technology High School is located in Napa Valley, California

DESCRIPTION OF PROGRAM

New Technology High School offers an innovative approach to a tech-prep curriculum in computer science and information systems. The school has a common core of rigorous coursework for the 11th and 12th grade. Instruction is totally interdisciplinary and project-based, with teachers coaching students individually and in work teams. All students engage in work-based education. Skill demonstration is assessed against published standards, demonstrated mastery, and displayed in individual student portfolios that also serve as employability portfolios. Graduation requirements include an Internship Class consisting of a classroom curriculum and unpaid work in technology, business, or education. All students are required to complete a minimum of four courses offered by Napa Valley College. They are expected to continue their technical education, continue at a two-year or four-year educational institution, or to join the workforce as a skilled worker. Students are able to obtain highly paid jobs while in high school or to support themselves as they continue their education.

New Tech uses Lotus Notes and Domino as the basis for all communication, eliminating the need for the numerous papers typical of most schools. Students receive instructions, policies, daily bulletins, and turn in assignments with this tool.

New Tech was created with help from Silicon Graphics to emulate the high technology business environment. Students are responsible for their own learning and that of others. Collaborative projects insure that as students succeed, they succeed together, each doing his or her part. Students have risen to the environment, showing respect for it, the numerous visitors, each other, and the staff.

New Tech enjoys the partnership of over 40 business, education, and community partners. The partners contribute time, resources, advice, products, and money. There were approximately 2,500 visitors in the 1996–97 school year.

SPECIAL OUTCOMES, RESULTS, AND ACCOMPLISHMENTS

New Technology High School, of Napa Valley Unified School District, is California's first digital high school. Its 200 students are juniors and seniors who reflect the multiethnic community in which they live. The school was created as a result of two problems in the community: an increased enrollment of 300 high school seniors, and the business community's detection of a severe lack of a regional workforce for high-technology industries. The business community contacted the school district and offered to assist in creating a high school of a new type. The result—New Technology High School—is referred to as "the school business built." The school was four years in the planning. The faculty and administration did not just want to add technology; they wanted to integrate it into every aspect of the curriculum and the building.

The students attend school in a business-like environment, each having their own Hewlett Packard desktop computer and access to scanners, digital cameras, laptops for home use, and full multimedia software.

New Tech uses its Web server as the basis for all communication, eliminating the need for the numerous papers typical of most schools. Among many other tasks, students receive instructions, policies, daily bulletins, and turn in assignments with this tool. All of the software is industry standard. They do not use special education software. Each student must pass a competency test in Office 97, as a graduation requirement.

The school is a recipient of a federally funded Tech Prep to demonstrate how it integrates technology with curriculum and work-skill building. The school will be hosting seminars and institutes for UC Berkeley, the California Technology Assistance Project, and Autodesk Project-Based Learning.

New Technology High School enjoys an active parent group, an advisory committee of business partners, a technology advisory committee, and an unparalleled educational partnership with Napa Community College.

Educational benefits from using technology are many. Teachers are able to put educational reform ideas into action to permit students to be self-learners and teachers to be facilitators because of the use of technology. Business partners offer professional development when they donate products. The school's tardy, truancy and attendance rates are better than the district average. CTBS scores and grades are also better than the district averages and improve as a student stays in the program. Student attitude, maturity, and respect for his or her environment are unlike any other public high school. Staff and students work longer hours because they like to. New Technology High School is a real community, not just a school.

DIFFICULTIES (ANTICIPATED AND UNANTICIPATED)

The greatest difficulties have been the cultural challenges presented to break the mold with educational reform initiatives. As with all pioneer efforts, the people involved were creative, hardworking, and risk takers. Even so, having a 1:1 student to PC ratio, full Internet connectivity, student e-mail accounts in and out of the building, operation in a business atmosphere, and over 40 business partners has stretched the limits of tolerance and educational norms. Resentment by other district high schools of New Tech's media exposure and resources has made recruitment of students difficult. Being a small focused program with connections to the two comprehensive high schools for athletics, fine arts, and foreign language has also hurt recruitment efforts.

THINGS TO CONSIDER

- Involve other schools in planning
- Build two-way business/education partnerships
- Budget significant dollars for professional development
- Be prepared to work long hours

♦ Recruit innovative, technology-friendly, hard-working faculty (all of New Tech's recruitment was via the Internet)

COSTS

Total cost is approximately $650,000
(all hardware, software, and training funds were raised through grants, philanthropic donation, and business/education partnerships)

CONTACT INFORMATION

Mark Morrison
Director
(707) 259-8557
(707) 259-8558 (Fax)
e-mail: Mark_Morrison@techhigh.napanet.net
http://www.nths.napa.ca.us

PROJECT CANALTREK

GOALS OF TECHNOLOGY PROGRAM

- ◆ To bring statewide reform and enhancement to the subject of Indiana history
- ◆ To demonstrate the value of telecommunications and the World Wide Web to teachers and students
- ◆ To involve pre-service teachers in hands-on classroom activities involving student-driven curriculum and technology

KEYWORDS

- ◆ History
- ◆ Internet
- ◆ Multimedia
- ◆ Telecommunications

LOCATION

Metropolitan School District of Perry Township
5401 S. Shelby Street
Indianapolis, IN 46227

DESCRIPTION OF SCHOOL AND COMMUNITY

Perry Township is the 10th largest K–12 public school district in Indiana and serves over 12,000 students. Included in this enrollment are approximately 1,200 students from the Indianapolis Public School system as part of a 1981 desegregation court order. The student population is composed of approximately 83% Caucasian, 2% Hispanic, Native American and Asian, and 15% African American.

The Metropolitan School District of Perry Township is located in the south central portion of Marion County, Indiana. The entire system is composed of nine elementary schools, the two largest middle schools in the state, two high schools, an alternative education program, and the RISE Learning Center for handicapped and disabled students.

DESCRIPTION OF PROGRAM

Project Canaltrek constitutes a statewide effort to bring reform and enhancement to the fourth grade subject of Indiana history, and to demonstrate to students and teachers the educational value of the World Wide Web. The project uses the historic Wabash-Erie Canal as a symbolic "information superhighway" to link students throughout the state in collaborative and educational relationships.

The project is student-centered and student-driven. Participants are asked to become familiar with their community to determine what makes it important in a historical context. Using the inquiry process, students ask questions about their community's historical significance and develop a research plan for one of these topics:

◆ Arts (folklore, literature, drama, music, etc.)

◆ People

◆ Events

◆ Resources (natural and/or man-made)

◆ Geography

◆ Economy/commerce

◆ Transportation

◆ Educational institutions

◆ Historical sites/tourism

◆ Local government

Students collect information regarding their topic using a variety of resources (including online resources). The information is developed into a multimedia presentation capable of being posted on the Project Canaltrek WWW site. The presentation in its entirety (text, graphics, artwork, sound, video, etc.) is sent via file transfer protocol (FTP), floppy disk, or CD-ROM to the Project Canaltrek staff members who arrange it for presentation on the Web.

For example, suppose a fourth grade classroom at Charles Elementary School in Richmond, Indiana decides to be part of the project. The teacher divides the classroom into small groups, and one of the groups decides they want to become experts on the Underground Railroad. The students determine what questions they would like to answer regarding their topic and then begin their research. Along the way, they revisit and revise their topic as needed. By the winter break, they have a sense of direction and begin to think about presenting their research findings on the Web site.

During the spring, the students collect materials for their multimedia presentation. They may take digitized images of the Levi Coffin House; create graphic artwork that outlines the Underground Railroad's common routes; attach informative text; and submit images of prominent abolitionists. Students then transfer this information to Web site "containers" that represent participant schools and that are arranged by topic on a graphical canal barge. The barge is steered by the project's fictitious and graphical guide, Fletcher McGee. Designing the Web site in this manner allows visitors to search by topic to learn more about Indiana history.

Project Canaltrek is also the perfect opportunity for those just entering the teaching profession to interact with students and guide them through the inquiry process. Pre-service teachers and their colleges or universities may even agree to help students with the technological elements of their presentations.

SPECIAL OUTCOMES, RESULTS, AND ACCOMPLISHMENTS

Project Canaltrek teachers cannot participate in the many project activities until they complete an online tutorial. The result of this tutorial is the education of many individuals throughout the state on the very basics of e-mail, attaching documentation to e-mail, joining listservs, visiting Web sites, downloading and uploading text and graphic files, and Web site design. The Indiana Department of Education realizes that technology is a viable tool for learning and, through Project Canaltrek, many teachers have access to very practical, project-specific information.

While it is still too early to tell, student participation in Project Canaltrek is expected to cause dramatic increases in test scores in specific areas of Indiana history and in the areas of English and humanities overall. Students are responsible for selecting very specific topics about their area, then using the inquiry process to whittle several topics down into one exclusive topic. Regular and pre-service teachers help the students with the inquiry process, but they allow students the freedom to choose their own topics. Once the research is done, the students are asked to prepare their findings in a multimedia format for posting on the Web. One main accomplishment of this activity is that students are encouraged to think in a different manner: they are asked to sort information and decide how it can best be displayed and conveyed. In this era of vast amounts of information, this skill is especially important for young people to learn.

Finally, pre-service teachers are typically in their first or second year of college and wondering whether education is the right choice for their career. Project Canaltrek schools are sought by colleges and universities in Indiana because pre-service teachers can be included in the project at any step of the process. They may guide students with the inquiry process and topic identification; they may assist with research and the accumulation of data; or they may make recommendations regarding display of the information. Pre-service teachers are in direct contact with the students and regular teachers during this process, and they are using technology as a tool for learning. These activities provide a very realistic picture of what an education career may look like once the pre-service teacher graduates and begins his or her career.

DIFFICULTIES (ANTICIPATED AND UNANTICIPATED)

Differing levels of technological competency and knowledge on the part of the teachers were anticipated, but the extent of the gulf between the competent and incompetent was not. Schools and teachers ranged from those able to design and maintain their own Web sites (so that the Project Canaltrek Web site merely provides a link), to those who have yet to obtain dedicated telephone lines. Because of such a wide spectrum, participation in Project Canaltrek is currently restricted to those teachers who have access to the Internet and e-mail through either their classroom or a computer lab.

While this may seem to be a negative aspect of the project, it is actually a positive aspect. Teachers now have a substantive reason to approach their principals, superintendents, and school boards and request online capability. They now have a statewide technology project to which they may direct their efforts, and they have a state-mandated topic (one that usually suffers in terms of test scores) to which their technology can be directed.

It is anticipated that, as more and more files come into the project office, the sheer burden of designing and maintaining the Web site will be a serious obstacle. One overall goal of the project is to make the Project Canaltrek Web site a clearinghouse for links to other Web sites set up by individual schools. This way, the schools themselves may design and control their Web sites, rather than depend upon the project staff to do so. However, very few schools in Indiana currently have the capability to manage their own Web sites, so for the next few years Project Canaltrek will have to take on that burden. It is impossible to determine how much of a problem the handling of all the separate files will be. However, it is safe to assume that as more and more schools sign on to the project, the need for dedicated personnel and/or time to manage the Web site will grow.

COSTS

The Indiana Department of Education awarded the MSD of Perry Township a $30,000 planning and implementation grant during the 1996–97 school year. These funds allowed for several meetings across the state, substitute teacher costs, consultant fees, and several pieces of technology equipment. For the pilot implementation year (the 1997–98 school year), that grant was increased by $20,000. This money translated into training on Web design for the project staff, additional meetings and equipment, as well as some regional training for teachers.

It costs nothing for a school or teacher to participate in Project Canaltrek, except for those pieces of equipment the teacher or school wants to purchase (digital camera, software, etc.). A teacher can participate in the project with nothing more than a camera. Any photos taken would be scanned by the project staff and posed on the Web; any text would be edited and copied to accompany the photos. Most teachers, however, have at their disposal digital cameras, microphones and software to produce sound files, and video cameras for digitized video files. It is anticipated that future costs will include regional training for project participants not only in the basic topics covered in the tutorial, but also in Web design, maintenance, and management.

CONTACT INFORMATION

Dennis M. Norris
Project Director, Project Canaltrek
(317) 780-4267
(317) 780-4265 (Fax)
e-mail: dnorris@iquest.net
http://www.msdpt.k12.in.us

RAIDERLINKS: AN INTEGRATED LAPTOP LEARNING PROGRAM

GOALS OF TECHNOLOGY PROGRAM

- To enhance student learning by integrating subject areas, and by incorporating computer-based technologies into daily lessons
- To utilize benefits of portable laptop computers to increase research abilities
- To enhance communication among students and teachers
- To reduce traditional fragmentation of knowledge and the segmentation of learning
- To focus on the academic and personal needs of students who are preparing themselves to live, study, and work in the twenty-first century

KEYWORDS

- Interdisciplinary learning
- Laptop computers
- Portfolio assessments

LOCATION

Thomas Jefferson High School
Federal Way School District
4248 South 288th
Auburn, WA 98001

DESCRIPTION OF SCHOOL AND COMMUNITY

- Grades 10–12
- Approximately 1,400 students and 65 teachers
- The facility is 30 years old (remodeled in 1990)

♦ Thomas Jefferson High School is located in a sub-
urb of Seattle and Tacoma. The school is predomi-
nantly Caucasian. The Raiderlinks program described here involved 55 students and 7 faculty
members in its first year (1996–97), and approximately 120 students and 14 faculty in its second
year (1997–98)

DESCRIPTION OF PROGRAM

Raiderlinks has as its overarching goal the enhancement
of student learning by integrating subject areas and incorporating computer-based technologies into daily lessons. Students and teachers involved in the project are each equipped
with their own personal laptop computer. Students in the
Raiderlinks project sign up for five core classes: Math, English, Social Studies, Science, and Computer Applications.
Students also sign up for one elective class. The team of teachers who developed and teach in the program meet regularly
to plan the use of instructional and study time, to coordinate
lessons, tasks, and projects, and to discuss the work and
progress of all the students in the program. The faculty team
works not only to instruct and coach, but also to serve as
model learners. The metaphors of "student as worker" and
"teacher as coach" pervade the program.

Raiderlinks differs greatly from the "traditional curriculum" of most high schools, even though it can be implemented with minimal alterations to traditional scheduling. It
is offered as a curricular option to students of all abilities. The
program establishes, as the heart of its curriculum, the teaching of skills and content knowledge while making its focus
the academic and personal needs of students who are preparing to live, study, and work in the 21st century. The curriculum depends on an interdisciplinary approach to learning the
subject matter, developing skills, and using teachers'
strengths.

The infusion of technology into an integrated curriculum
provides a model that can be replicated in almost any junior
and senior high school. The pilot project was implemented
during the 1996–97 school year, though parts of the program
had been piloted during previous years. The laptop-based

curriculum is designed for three years with progressively greater flexibility.

SPECIAL OUTCOMES, RESULTS, AND ACCOMPLISHMENTS

Although not constrained by curricular pressure from advanced placement programs or achievement testing, students do continue the normal sequence of standardized testing for college, vocational school, or admission to military. Students take the PSAT, SAT I, SAT II, ACT, and AP tests in a traditional pattern if their individual learning plans call for these results. Various software programs are used to accelerate the test preparation process and raise the level of performance by any student on any given exam. Laptop computers allow students in the Raiderlinks Project to access these programs from the classroom, or through any telephone line.

Raiderlinks depends fundamentally on utilizing technology in learning. Learning assessments are aimed toward exhibitions and other demonstrations of skill and mastery. The project uses electronic portfolio assessment, student-directed research, classroom discussion, and rigorous performance expectations. The ability to use computers and networks as tools for communicating, solving problems, and gaining access to information is a principal focus. Students also develop the ability to use multimedia tools to present creative exhibitions of their knowledge. Math and writing abilities are positively impacted by the incorporation of the laptops.

DIFFICULTIES (ANTICIPATED AND UNANTICIPATED)

Finding time for all of the teachers to meet is a major obstacle. Often meetings are held outside of the school day.

The curriculum needs to be rewritten to incorporate the subject areas and the computer. This requires open communication among the faculty and time to develop the new curriculum.

One anticipated difficulty that did not materialize was damaged or stolen computers. Of the 62 laptops that were used the first year, only 2 required repairs. None were stolen.

THINGS TO CONSIDER

The classroom teacher continues to be the critical variable for student learning. Computer technology is a tool to enhance learning. The teacher must possess the vision and motivation for using this tool.

Establish connections with local lending institutions (for computer loans), computer hardware companies, and software companies to defer costs and keep systems upgraded.

COSTS

Students agree to purchase a laptop computer, complete with the software and connectivity requirements (e.g., Ethernet cards, modem, etc.). Payment plans allow this purchase to span the three years they attend the high school. To allow equal access for all students, the district may purchase some laptops and loan them to students. The district technology budget provides each participating faculty member with a laptop computer.

Hardware and software: $1,800–$2,400/computer
Training: $1,000

CONTACT INFORMATION

Bruce E. Larson
Assistant Professor, Western Washington University
(360) 650-3702
(360) 650-7516 (Fax)
e-mail: blarson@wce.wwu.edu

Joseph Gotchy
Teacher-Social Studies, Thomas Jefferson High School
(253) 839-7490
(253) 941-6857 (Fax)
e-mail: Joe-Gotchy@FWSD.wednet.edu

Bruce Case
Teacher-Computer Applications, Thomas Jefferson
  High School
(253) 839-7490
(253) 941-6857 (Fax)
e-mail: Bruce-Case@FWSD.wednet.edu

READ MY HANDS

GOALS OF TECHNOLOGY PROGRAM

- To increase the reading and language skills
- To increase communication skills in a language other than English
- To increase computer and multimedia skills
- To increase self-esteem

KEYWORDS

- Exceptional education
- Language arts
- Multimedia
- Reading

LOCATION

Osceola Middle School
526 SE Tuscawilla Avenue
Ocala, FL 34471

DESCRIPTION OF SCHOOL AND COMMUNITY

- Grades 6–8
- Approximately 1,128 students and 43 teachers
- The school facility was built in 1924 and is a historic building
- Osceola Middle School is located in Ocala, Florida. The student population is approximately 76% Caucasian, 18% African American, 4% Hispanic, and 2% Asian. The Ocala/Marion County area has a broad economic base that is supported by light industry, agriculture, tourism and manufacturing

DESCRIPTION OF PROGRAM

Read My Hands gives both regular education and deaf/hard-of-hearing middle school students the opportunity to create, illustrate, and publish their own original multimedia stories and reports using HyperStudio software. When the stories and reports are complete, they add a movie of a person signing the text on each page. These are then shared with other regular education, deaf/hard-of-hearing, learning disabled, and language-impaired elementary, middle, and high school students.

The students create their projects on a Power Macintosh 5260 with 24MB RAM, and a video in/out card added. They use HyperStudio to produce their projects. To incorporate any printed material (noncopyrighted) or photographs, they use a scanner. When their project is grammatically correct and illustrated, they then add sign language. Regular education, hearing students learn the necessary sign language vocabulary to add to their project by using American Sign Language Dictionaries and the assistance of the deaf/hard-of-hearing students. A video recording is made of the author signing each sentence in the story, which recording is added to the story. When the project is complete, it is published. Using an external hard drive, the story or report is given to another elementary school to be loaded on its computers.

At the elementary, middle, and high schools, other deaf/hard-of-hearing students, regular education students, language impaired students, and learning disabled students are able to enjoy the creative fictional stories and innovative reports. The middle school students are able to showcase the knowledge they have gained as a result of creating their multimedia projects.

SPECIAL OUTCOMES, RESULTS, AND ACCOMPLISHMENTS

- ♦ Increased communication between the deaf/hard-of-hearing students and regular education students

- ◆ Enhanced student motivation, communication, and cooperation between special education teacher and regular education teachers
- ◆ Increased knowledge of technology and multimedia. The students used this knowledge in other core curriculum areas to create projects and reports for mainstream classes
- ◆ Increased self-esteem as the special education students became the experts at something they could share with hearing students
- ◆ Other teachers have become interested in duplicating this type of project
- ◆ This project received the Little Red School House John Gardner Award

DIFFICULTIES (ANTICIPATED AND UNANTICIPATED)

The external hard drive did not always perform as well as expected. Another difficulty, although it was a benefit as well, was that other teachers at Osceola became so interested in the project that they wanted to send students to the ESE classroom throughout the day. They used participation in the project as a reward for their students.

THINGS TO CONSIDER

Adding quicktime movies of sign language caused the stacks to be very large. Therefore, it was necessary to use an external hard drive to distribute the stacks to other interested teachers.

COSTS

Zip 100 external drive	$150
Apple external AV card	$100
16MB SIMM	$100
HyperStudio software	$105

The school provided the classroom with a Power Macintosh 5260 for the project. The scanner and digital camera were used in another regular education teacher's classroom. A scanner can be purchased for $400 or less, and a Casio Digital camera for approximately $360. Currently, a Power Macintosh 5400/180 is $1,500. There were no operational costs involved.

CONTACT INFORMATION

Victoria Rath
Teacher of the Deaf/Hard of Hearing
(352) 622-5171 or (352) 401-0282
(352) 840-5735 (Fax)
e-mail: vorath@praxis.net

SENIOR CITIZENS + STUDENTS = POWERFUL LEARNING

GOALS OF TECHNOLOGY PROGRAM

- To develop problem-solving and critical thinking strategies
- To improve basic academic skills
- To encourage community involvement
- To develop technological literacy
- To enhance student confidence and self-esteem
- To provide one-on-one tutoring

KEYWORDS

- Critical thinking
- Internet
- Senior citizens

LOCATION

North Dover Elementary
Toms River Regional Schools
1759 New Hampshire Avenue
Toms River, NJ 08795

DESCRIPTION OF SCHOOL AND COMMUNITY

- Grades K–6
- Approximately 850 students and 50 teachers
- Facility is approximately 35 years old with several additional areas
- Suburban school district with over 17,000 pupils, K–12, in 11 elementary, 2 intermediate and 3 high schools. Students are primarily Caucasian with

some African American students as well as individuals from India, Pakistan, and Puerto Rico

DESCRIPTION OF PROGRAM

This project creates a collaborative learning environment where elementary students and senior citizens work together. Students attend classes in the technology lab weekly beginning in third grade. The curriculum affords experiences in many areas of technology: word processing, desktop publishing, databases, spreadsheets, drawing, telecommunications, and computer applications (with video cameras, CD-ROM, and LEGO/LOGO integration).

This project creates a collaborative learning environment where elementary students and senior citizens work together.
© Clare Devine

May is National Intergenerational Month. Through a local senior citizens publication, *The Lighthouse*, a group of senior citizens are identified who are interested in becoming computer literate. *The Lighthouse* is sent to over 40,000 people.

Usually classes include about 20–25 senior participants. Senior guests come to the technology lab and are teamed up one-on-one with sixth-grade students. From applications and projects learned during the year, students share their expertise. Class begins with introductions and word processing.

As a word processing project, seniors are asked to type an essay about any invention that was made during their life and that altered their lives. Topics have included "Where Were You in WWII?," "My Life as a Teenager," and "My Elementary School Days." When possible, these stories are collected and a booklet of everyone's story is made.

These are printed and handed out during the last class. Subsequent weeks include desktop publishing, databases, and using the Internet.

An Internet database is being developed to keep information about "senior memories." Anyone in the world can write about their memories and recollections. The initial site will be at CPAW (Computer Pals Across the World) in Australia (http://www2.hawkesbury.uws.edu.au/CPAW).

The interaction involves real-world learning and instruction. Both groups participate in problem solving, critical thinking, and cross-aged social and team skills.

SPECIAL OUTCOMES, RESULTS, AND ACCOMPLISHMENTS

Student and senior-guest rapport developed, with both groups changing perceptions.

Students met older people who still work to learn new things. Seniors were impressed with student skills and demeanor. The computer became a vehicle for better understanding between generations.

Senior guests learned new skills in the field of technology. The course is free, and senior citizens are directly benefiting from public school taxes. Students build self-esteem and begin to realize that many of their skills are useful and sought after by others. Slower students are the most eager participants.

The CPAW Web site will become a repository of personal history written by senior citizens, or anyone of any age. The school hopes to see the archives grow and develop into organized, specific areas. The initial areas are: Advertising,

Fashion, Customs, Food, War, Leisure, Home Life, Transport, Media, Health, Law and Order, Energy, and Employment. The essays submitted will dictate other areas and subtopics within each category. The intergenerational input focuses on comparisons. These similarities and differences will create a database of perspectives from around the world.

DIFFICULTIES (ANTICIPATED AND UNANTICIPATED)

Accomplishing this project had few difficulties and many rewards. Students, taking the role of tutors, must learn to share what they know in an organized, relevant fashion. There may be problems with the logistics of parking and with handicapped seniors needing special services. Make school officials aware of senior guests in the building and avoid fire drills during visits. A ratio of 1 senior per 1.5 students promotes flexibility. There may be one or two students who need help or who are not interested in participating in the project. A surprising problem with this project is that not all adults write well. Editing can be difficult to accomplish diplomatically without hurting a guest's ego.

THINGS TO CONSIDER

- ◆ Teachers should not handle registration
- ◆ Logistics of parking and distance to the classrooms should be given careful consideration
- ◆ Avoid visits when student, bus, or other traffic is especially heavy

COSTS

No additional costs were incurred in this program.

CONTACT INFORMATION

Clare Devine
(732) 505-5860
(732) 914-9706 (Fax)
e-mail: cdevine@csionline.com

SIGNALS PROJECT
(SUPPLEMENTAL INSTRUCTION FOR GIRLS IN THE NAUTICAL APPLICATIONS FOR LEARNING SCIENCE)

GOALS OF TECHNOLOGY PROGRAM

- To address the problem of female underrepresentation in science-related fields
- To use technology to establish educational and inspirational relationships with female scientists of the United States Coast Guard, United States Navy, and other marine environment science institutions
- To provide a leadership model for females that increases their interest and ownership in science and builds confidence in their ability to be real scientists

KEYWORDS

- Leadership
- Military
- Science
- Telecommunications

LOCATION

Southport Middle School
5715 S. Keystone Avenue
Indianapolis, IN 46227

DESCRIPTION OF SCHOOL AND COMMUNITY

The SIGNALS Project has been conducted the last three years solely within Southport Middle School, which is the second largest middle school in the state of Indiana with a student population of 1,500. The school includes grades 6–8, and there are 9 teachers involved in the project (yet all 80 teachers assist in some manner).

The Metropolitan School District of Perry Township is located in the south central portion of Marion County, Indiana. The population of Perry Township is in excess of 80,000. The district serves over 12,000 students in grades K–12, making the district the tenth largest in the state. Included in this enrollment are approximately 1,200 students from the Indianapolis Public School system as part of a 1981 desegregation court order.

The student enrollment is comprised of approximately 83% White, 2% Hispanic, Native American, and Asian, and 15% African American. The entire system is comprised of nine elementary schools, the two largest middle schools in the state, two high schools, an alternative education program, and the RISE Learning Center for handicapped and disabled students. Eleventh and twelfth grade students may attend the Central Nine area vocational/technical school.

The district is a member of the Indiana School Study Council, and all schools are fully accredited by the Indiana Department of Education. The high schools are members of the North Central Association of Colleges and Secondary Schools, the Indiana High School Athletic Association, and, along with the middle schools, the Indiana School Principals Association, Division of Student Activities. The mission of the school district is:

> Students are our priority. The Metropolitan School District of Perry Township commits to promoting equitable, appropriate learning in an excellent educational environment. We pledge to challenge our students to acquire the knowledge and to master the skills necessary for lifelong success.

DESCRIPTION OF PROGRAM

The SIGNALS Project (Supplemental Instruction for Girls in the Nautical Applications for Learning Science) is an effort to address the problem of female underrepresentation in the science-related fields. In a collaborative relationship between the Metropolitan School District of Perry Township, the United States Navy, the United States Coast Guard, and various other marine science institutions, female scientists from across the country provide educational and inspirational supplements to the standard middle school science curriculum. Although the project is guided by middle school science teachers, it is directed by a selected group of female students known as the SIGNALS Officer Corps. The Officer Corps represents the different ranks and responsibilities similar to those of a shipboard environment, and the project is run with a high degree of discipline, pride, integrity, and teamwork.

There are four headings to The SIGNALS Project under which each of the goals and objectives are listed:

- ◆ Scientific Fundamentals
- ◆ Inspirational
- ◆ Concrete
- ◆ Leadership

The objectives under the Scientific Fundamentals seek to make students aware of the practical applications of science, and of the possibility of integrating science into other curricular areas. Students engage in the process of scientific research and methods, and find ways to integrate the project into other areas of the curriculum. The Inspirational heading provides female students contact with female scientists who serve as role models and inspirational mentors. Students conduct activities that are conducive to inspirational thought and action. Under Concrete, students are allowed to conduct hands-on, self-directed learning to increase confidence and knowledge. They are expected to perform a number of tasks involving manipulation of audio, video, telecommunications and distance learning equipment. Finally, Leadership offers students a chance to maintain a level and manner of behavior that is modeled after nautical military and scientific tradi-

tions. Through the SIGNALS Officer Corps, project participants are able to take control of their learning and their relationships with other teachers and students. All objectives
directly focus on increasing female students' sense of self-
confidence and positive attitude towards science; areas
which current research shows have a direct impact upon the
problem of female underrepresentation.

Evaluation of The SIGNALS Project is done by both the
SIGNALS Officer Corps and the science teachers. Participants
are expected to keep weekly journals, pass uniform inspec-
tions, give professional presentations, and maintain exemplary standards. By involving female students directly and
giving them a sense of ownership in their learning, the project
attains levels of self-confidence and positive attitude that
carry over to the high school years and beyond. As the library
of contacts with female scientists grows, the SIGNALS Project
becomes a source by which other schools use the established
network of resources to supplement their own science curricula. This type of educational/inspirational interaction proves
invaluable to students who have little or no knowledge of female contributions to science, and no reference point from
which to construct their own career goals. The project also
helps erase common misconceptions about female capabilities and expectations in today's complex society.

SPECIAL OUTCOMES, RESULTS, AND
ACCOMPLISHMENTS

Under the Scientific Fundamentals element, it has become apparent that those females participating in the project
become extremely familiar with the science curriculum and
how it can be integrated with other topics. Skills are highly
developed in terms of developing hypotheses, using variable
data, investigating methodologies, and reaching conclusions.
At the end of each grading period, members of the SIGNALS
Officer Corps must present three specific and clearly written
statements demonstrating what they have learned about scientific research through involvement with the project.

The Inspirational element has proven to be the most dramatic in terms of accomplishments. Whenever a female scientist is contacted to supplement the standard science cur-

riculum with practical and useful examples, she is also asked to furnish a short biography about herself. Nearly every female scientist states that she hated science early on, but once she got into middle school there were one or two teachers who sparked such an interest in science that she chose it for a career. When middle school girls hear this message it is very powerful. They believe they can truly make a difference, and that the world is open to them so far as career choices are concerned.

The Concrete element of the project has also produced astounding results. The female participants very quickly become adept at all aspects of the technology: operating audio/visual equipment; navigating the Internet and the World Wide Web; uploading and downloading text and graphics; sending e-mail with documents attached; storing data and information; manipulating distance learning equipment and establishing satellite links. They are also required to construct a computer-generated presentation as part of their ability to move up through the Officer Corps ranks. Their work in this area has been extremely creative and effective, causing more and more girls to join its ranks.

Finally, under the Leadership element, the SIGNALS Officer Corps is a quasimilitary organization requiring the maintenance of a uniform and performance ribbons/awards; the maintenance of a journal; knowledge of a project credo; and participation in team-building exercises. The US Coast Guard and US Navy have been so impressed with this program that they have asked the project's creator and director, Mr. Dennis Norris, to establish a national model that is replicable in other schools across the nation. The result of the Leadership element, quite simply, is the creation of a corps of females who are quite serious about bringing science into their lives and who use a military, nautical, and shipboard ethos to direct their efforts.

DIFFICULTIES (ANTICIPATED AND UNANTICIPATED)

One anticipated difficulty was designing the project so it was not exclusionary to male students. This problem, however, has not surfaced. Males are included in all classroom activities and are able to see the female scientists' curriculum supplements and inspirational messages. The only exclusionary element of the project is the SIGNALS Officer Corps, for which only female students are recruited. Male students have expressed an appreciation for the project, seeing a need for females to take ownership of science and view it as a possible career choice.

An unanticipated problem was the popularity of the project, especially membership into the SIGNALS Officer Corps. Only a certain number of participants are needed to learn and operate the technology, or to contact female scientists. The management and logistics of the project have shown the need to expand the activities of the Officer Corps to include many other things. That task is currently underway and it is anticipated that more community service opportunities will be available, as well as opportunities to bring local female scientists into the classroom.

COSTS

In 1996, The SIGNALS Project was given the Pioneering Partners Award by the Pioneering Partners Foundation and Ameritech, which named it as one of the best technology projects in the Great Lakes States region. Funding from the award allowed the project staff to disseminate the project at various conferences, and it brought in much-needed supplies. The project has received minimal grant monies, yet it has not aggressively sought grant funds since its inception. It tends to run on its own through donations and small contributions.

As the project expands the costs are increasing. The SIGNALS Officer Corps wears a uniform and ribbons/medals are awarded for outstanding performance. There are also costs associated with contacting female scientists and maintaining the technology equipment. So far, these costs have been kept to a minimum. Beyond that, the project can be replicated for very little cost. The national model will be completed by the end of the 1997–98 school year and will explain to interested schools how to keep their costs down.

CONTACT INFORMATION

Maureen McCune, Project Coordinator
7th Grade Science Teacher
Southport Middle School
5715 S. Keystone Avenue
Indianapolis, IN 46277

Dennis M. Norris, Project Director
The SIGNALS Project
Metropolitan School District of Perry Township
5401 S. Shelby Street
Indianapolis, IN 46227
(317) 7800-4267
(317) 780-4265 (Fax)
e-mail: dnorris@iquest.net

SPACE SHUTTLE SIMULATION LABORATORY

GOALS OF TECHNOLOGY PROGRAM

- To develop and operate a computer-based simulation laboratory that models the use of NASA data, images, and Web sites within the context of a typical K–12 school curriculum
- To develop interactive curriculum models

KEYWORDS

- Internet
- Multimedia
- Simulation

LOCATION

College of Education
University of Nebraska at Omaha
60th and Dodge Streets
Omaha, NE 68182

DESCRIPTION OF SCHOOL AND COMMUNITY

- College of Education has 66 full-time and 134 part-time faculty with 1,500 undergraduate and 838 graduate students within education majors
- College works closely with Metropolitan Omaha Education Consortium of 90,000 students
- Urban institution with numerous K–12 collaborative programs
- Focused goals for educational technology integration and multicultural efforts

DESCRIPTION OF PROGRAM

The Space Shuttle Simulation Laboratory, through the leadership of faculty from the Department of Teacher Education in the College of Education, is a collaborative effort with other university departments (Aviation and Physics) and K–12 practitioners. The primary purpose of the laboratory is to respond to the need for interactive curriculum models, and to train teachers in the use of such models by building on the motivational content of space flight. These curriculum models provide active learning experiences for pre-service and in-service education, and incorporate constructivism, project-oriented learning, interdisciplinary learning, and active learning.

The Space Shuttle Simulation Laboratory has of three major components. The first is a partial replica of the space shuttle Challenger. This component contains a flight deck for two and workspace for six others in a space immediately behind the flight deck. The second component is the Mission Control Area. This component contains furniture resembling the actual Mission Control, and 10 computer workstations. The third component is a Briefing and Image Processing Room that contains seating for 40 students, six computer imaging stations, work tables, a large screen display device, and various reference materials. All computer workstations are networked and have Internet access. (See figures on page 195.)

A file server supports this project by providing intranet and Internet access. In addition, the file server supports software for local Web sites, Internet Web sites, HyperStudio stacks, video, and graphics. A large percentage of the related software was developed and written collaboratively by professors, teachers, and graduate students. All software facilitates remote access from the World Wide Web, so that participating classes can also use the simulation software off-site.

All shuttle lab activities revolve around NASA-based role-playing, and incorporate real NASA data and images. This includes the use of NASA-developed curriculum related to the Center for the Application of Space Data in Education (CASDE) and the KidSat program (remote control of external cameras on the real NASA Shuttle flights). In addition, the lab

All computer workstations are networked and have Internet access.
© Space Shuttle Simulation Laboratory

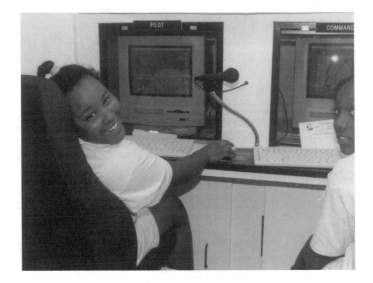

The curriculum modules provide active learning experiences that
incorporate constructivism, project-oriented learning, and
interdisciplinary learning.
© Space Shuttle Simulation Laboratory

makes heavy use of the NASA hands-on curriculum activities, NASA Web Sites, and Mission to Planet Earth tech-
nology-based lessons. Also, several visits and official collaborative activities have already been conducted with NASA.

The interdisciplinary nature of the simulated shuttle missions supports instruction in mathematics, science, reading,
and writing. Initially, shuttle lab simulations were developed
for grades 5 through 9. Additional missions for secondary
students and adults are expected to be developed later. Teachers in elementary and secondary schools, undergraduate and
graduate students in teacher education, and professors are
being trained in using the developed integrated curriculum
models. In the future, missions could also be developed for
parents, community leaders, and the business community.

All shuttle lab activities, missions, and visits are part of a
larger teacher-facilitated unit. A typical mission starts in the
students' classroom with a premission briefing that follows a
prepared curriculum outline. Following this introductory
phase, students are transported to the university where they
undergo a second briefing session. Students are divided into
three groups: one group is assigned to the shuttle, another
group is assigned to the space imaging center, and the third
group assigned to Mission Control. Following the mission,
students assigned to each room exchange places, allowing all
students to work within each environment. At the conclusion
of the missions, students engage in follow-up debriefing exercises beginning at the university and continuing at their respective classrooms.

SPECIAL OUTCOMES, RESULTS, AND ACCOMPLISHMENTS

- Identified as a National Science Foundation Center for Excellence in Teaching and Learning
- Strong collaborative participation by local schools,
  particularly schools with a high percentage of minority students
- Established as a satellite distribution center for
  the Eisenhower National Clearinghouse

♦ Participant in the NASA KidSat program, which includes the remote Internet access of cameras aboard several NASA Space Shuttle Missions

DIFFICULTIES (ANTICIPATED AND UNANTICIPATED)

The activities to be conducted within the Space Shuttle Simulation lab and follow-up integration activities necessitate that the facility is well coordinated, scheduled, and operated on an ongoing basis. This requires a more permanent budget for the operational and personnel costs related to this unique facility. Currently, the operational budget is drawn from several temporary grant projects focused on use of the facility; however, expectations for long-term operation necessitate a more permanent funding structure. In addition to funding challenges, various software and hardware advancements are demanding a continuous and periodic refinement of the simulation software within the facility in order to embrace the newest capabilities of Internet-based technologies.

THINGS TO CONSIDER

♦ Purchase equipment that is significantly Internet capable with regard to memory and speed

♦ Incorporate considerable joint planning, which involves interested professionals at both the K–12 and University levels

♦ Contact local businesses for possible discounts and donations related to the purchase of facility components

♦ Ensure that all curriculum-related materials are Internet accessible

COSTS

Hardware	$100,000
Software	$20,000
Training	$10,000
Operations	$70,000 (per year)

CONTACT INFORMATION

Dr. Neal Grandgenett
Associate Professor of Mathematics Education
(402) 554-2690
(402) 554-3491 (Fax)
e-mail: grandgen@unomaha.edu

Dr. Neal Topp
Assistant Professor of Educational Technology
(402) 554-2435
(402) 554-3491 (Fax)
e-mail: topp@unomaha.edu

Dr. Robert Mortenson
Associate Dean–College of Education
(402) 554-2719
(402) 554-3491 (Fax)
e-mail: morten@unomaha.edu

Dr. Elliott Ostler
Assistant Professor of Mathematics Education
(402) 554-3486
(402) 554-3491 (Fax)
e-mail: eostler@unomaha.edu

Dr. Carol Mitchell
Assistant Professor of Science Education
(402) 554-2428
(402) 554-3491 (Fax)
e-mail: ctmitch@unomaha.edu

STUDY AMERICAN HISTORY, STUDY YOUR HISTORY

GOALS OF TECHNOLOGY PROGRAM

- To have students gain a greater appreciation of both their own history and American History through the use of technology and integrated language arts and Social Studies curricular units

KEYWORDS

- Curriculum integration
- History
- Language arts

LOCATION

Ladysmith Middle School
115 East 6th Street
Ladysmith, WI 54848

DESCRIPTION OF SCHOOL AND COMMUNITY

- Grades 6–8
- Approximately 250 students and 18 classroom teachers
- The school is a 70-year-old brick building that has seen many changes and additions. Ladysmith is a community of 4,000 people located in rural northwest Wisconsin. Rusk County has one of the highest unemployment rates and lowest per capita income levels in Wisconsin. Forestry and agriculture are the primary businesses of the area, although tourism and light industry are increasing. The community is approximately 90% Caucasian and 5% Asian

DESCRIPTION OF PROGRAM

Innovative integrated curricular units allow students to gain a greater appreciation of their own history and American History by combining technology, research, writing, speaking, and reenactment. These units cover the American Revolution, immigration and genealogy, and the American Civil War. The units last three-quarters of the school year. The most effective way to describe the units is to examine one in greater detail.

The second of the three units involves an immigration and genealogy unit to be undertaken in language arts, which includes first and second generation interviews and investigations into the student's own ancestry. The use of computerized genealogy programs is encouraged. Students later present the results of their research.

A study of the immigration patterns of the mid-19th Century also begins. Although all students are not able to research their own history, they can become honorary Irish. Students utilize an updated version of the Harvard E.T.C. Irish Immigrant Adventure. They utilize a multimedia presentation on the Irish immigrants, and write a journal from the perspective of their adopted Irish family. More capable students are encouraged to create a multimedia journal.

Howard Gardner's multiple intelligence theories are utilized in the American Revolution and Civil War units through the numerous learning styles addressed and in the students' research projects. Students can choose from a variety of research and product modalities including primary source research, on- and off-line research, formal essay writing, fiction writing, drawing, modeling/sculpting, dramatic writing and live or video production, game creation, and multimedia production. Many students combine another product type with multimedia because of the flexibility it offers in presentation.

SPECIAL OUTCOMES, RESULTS, AND ACCOMPLISHMENTS

- ♦ Improved comprehension and retention of knowledge, resulting from technology and integrated

language arts and history, addresses many different learning styles

♦ Development of higher-order cognitive skills

♦ Increased parent involvement, especially during
immigration/genealogy unit

♦ Increased interest in reading by students

♦ Increased interest/attention by at-risk students

♦ A greater appreciation by students of both their
own history and American History, a stronger
feeling for who they are and what has come before them, and a personal meaning of history is
gained

DIFFICULTIES (ANTICIPATED AND UNANTICIPATED)

The varied level of student ability is always a challenge to
the teacher, but especially so when teaching new concepts
and activities on a computer. This must be planned for and
additional tutorial time must be anticipated when doing
whole-class computer activities.

Integrating two separate classes and providing both combined and separate activities was initially complicated by
class schedules. A willing teacher team and a flexible principal allowed sufficient changes to provide significant flexibility in the integration planning.

COSTS

A sufficient number of computers for student research,
project development, and simulations is essential. A number
equal to one-half a class is minimum. The program involves
four classes of 20–24 with a dedicated lab of 12 computers.
This tends to be adequate except when projects are due.

Approximately: $25,000

ClarisWorks is used for most word processing, spreadsheet, database work, some presentations, and for the Irish
Immigrant simulation.

Approximately: $500

Other software: MECC's Wagon Train (a networked form
of Oregon Trail), multiple copies of Grolier's Encyclopedia

and Multi-Educator's Revolutionary War, Civil War, and American History CD-ROM's, several additional different Revolutionary War and Civil War CD-ROM's, and other research/information programs.

Approximately: $3,000

Curriculum development and training time for participating teachers.

Approximately: $5,000

CONTACT INFORMATION

Todd Novakofski
(715) 532-5252
(715) 532-7455 (Fax)
e-mail: toddnova@centuryinter.net

TECHNOLOGY INTEGRATION STAFF-DEVELOPMENT MODELS THAT WORK TOWARD SYSTEMIC CHANGE

GOALS OF TECHNOLOGY PROGRAM

- To provide K–12 teachers with the technology and training necessary to allow them to work toward integrating technology seamlessly into their curriculum
- To strengthen student learning for real-world applications
- To allow students to compete at the highest levels nationally

KEYWORDS

- Multimedia
- Staff development
- Telecommunications

LOCATION

Orange County Public Schools
Teacher Academy
445 West Amelia Street
Orlando, FL 32801

DESCRIPTION OF SCHOOL AND COMMUNITY

- Grades K–12 and alternative instructional centers
- Approximately 132,000 students in district
- Approximately 8,828 teachers and support personnel

- Facility structures range from newly constructed to 50 years old; Orange County Public Schools is the 16th largest school district in the United States and the 5th largest in Florida
- The area's major industry is tourism and newer high-tech industries are growing in the community. The school district population represents 200 countries with 119 different languages and dialects spoken. Approximately 49% are Caucasian, 29% African American, 18% Hispanic, 3% Asian and Pacific Islanders, and less than 1% Native American. Forty percent of the student population receives free or reduced lunch services

DESCRIPTION OF PROGRAM

With all the expectations of teachers, there is little time to learn how to use new technologies. Research has shown that it will be at least ten years before enough teachers are technologically "savvy" enough for technology to be integrated into the general curriculum and day-to-day instruction. Effective training models suggest the idea of "relevant" training for teachers. They are designed to give teachers and students skills that can be used in the creation of authentic student products. If both students and teachers become knowledgeable about how to use the technology to meet various instructional needs, then the skills developed will have relevancy for everyone involved. As more teachers turn their classrooms into student-centered environments and students take on the responsibility for creating their own knowledge, this type of instruction, with continued follow-up support, can help teachers change their instructional model and methods.

The models presented here have in common that:

- Each teacher involved in the summer program is paid a $50 per day stipend
- Each teacher is awarded in-service credit toward credential renewal
- Each teacher is allowed follow-up access to summer workshop leaders

♦ Each teacher is given a multimedia computer for his or her classroom with a full assortment of the software necessary for project construction. (In the secondary model, students are awarded a semester credit for their participation.)

In addition, teachers can borrow and use in their classrooms several Alpha Smart units, digital cameras or ROVER, a wheeled case containing six laptop computers.

In one implemented staff development model, middle and high school teachers and students learn to create multimedia products in a two-week summer institute. Each team selected to participate consists of one teacher and two students, who will be in the teacher's class in the fall. They are given instruction in a variety of software programs and computer basics that help them with their projects. If the group of participants is large enough, technology-skilled high school students are hired to help with the instruction. Some group instruction is provided but the majority of the instruction is provided using the concept of "each-one teach-one."

A group theme is presented and each team works on a specific part of the larger project. One summer group created a CD-ROM about the different animals in the local zoo. Each school-based team was assigned a different zoo animal for its project. A group field trip was made to the zoo where students and teachers talked with animal caretakers and photographed and recorded information about their animals. They planned out their projects, used the Internet for research, and then created the projects.

At the end of the workshop, principals, community members, and other guests were invited to view all the projects on display and to use a variety of instruments to evaluate the projects. Team members took turns staffing their group's station and spent the rest of their time viewing and evaluating other team projects. The zoo project was comprised of 45 multimedia teams. At the end of the two-week period, teachers walk away with a CD-ROM containing all the work of all the teams.

A second model for elementary teachers in grades 3 to 5 uses a slightly different approach. First, the teachers spend a week together learning how to use their new computer, multimedia software applications, Internet, and e-mail, and are introduced to a variety of possible projects and approaches. They also meet with identified mentor teachers who help with the tough issues such as time management. Once the school year begins, each teacher returns for additional training, but this time they come with their entire class for a three-hour, intensive HyperStudio basics session. If the lab does not have enough computers for each student to have his or her own, then additional laptops are brought in for the instruction. Volunteers, interns, and staff are stationed around the classroom to help students with directions as the instruction is given. This session is designed to bring the skill sets required for creating multimedia projects for the entire class to a higher level.

The class returns for a second instructional session during the second semester. This time the instruction is of the teacher's choice. Teachers can design their own session or choose from things like advanced HyperStudio, Internet research, Web page construction, or project construction time. Teachers are also asked to attend four follow-up staff development days during the school year—one day during each of the four grading periods. Sessions address topics such as barriers that are keeping them from moving forward with technology use in their classroom, intervention strategies, sharing of projects they have begun to work on, consulting with mentor teachers, addressing time-management issues and broadening their support network.

Teachers from both models presented above can request additional on-site help with special problems. The summer instruction is a great way to get teachers and students started using technology in their curriculum. Follow-up beyond the initial workshop is key to helping teachers create true technology integration and systemic change.

ROVER COME OVER

Teachers' time constraints continue to be among the major roadblocks to learning to use new technologies. Orange County is providing instruction for teachers and students together in the "multimedia you can make yourself" program HyperStudio. This model provides an expedient way to help teachers infuse technology into their curriculum because they do not have to be expert users before they begin working with their students. Teachers receive "Next Steps" instruction as they need it instead of canned presentations at inappropriate times. They have opportunities to practice with their students "giving back to their community."

HyperStudio was selected as the shell for their projects because it is a cross-platform, inexpensive authoring tool, and can be taught to any ability level, child to adult. The software can be as simple or as sophisticated as needed. It allows the students to make decisions and to focus on the project content rather than the construction tool and software.

Phase One: Rover Comes to Visit

Rover is a special portable computer case that travels to schools with a multimedia instructor to provide additional computers and instruction. (See photograph on page 208.) The curriculum is customized for each teacher and class as needed, and gives the class a headstart in learning to use HyperStudio.

Rover is a 75-pound, rolling computer case that contains six laptop computers, mice, power strips, and cleaning supplies. Rover travels to different schools to provide instruction and makes extended visits for project work. Each computer in the case is named after a pet and has the pet's picture on the desktop. This helps the instructor to keep up with machine problems and helps students intimidated by technology to understand that each computer is a little different and might act just a little different than the next one. If Rover visits a school without the instructor for an extended period of time, the naming helps the students tell the instructor which computers are misbehaving.

Most of the time teachers feel they must become experts in a software package before they introduce it to the students. In this situation, each participant takes back something different they have learned. The strength in this type of training is the teacher learns with the students and all learners are "the expert" when they return to a daily routine. No substitute or transportation to an outside facility is required.

Rover is a special portable computer case that travels to
schools with a multimedia instructor to provide additional
computers and instruction.
© Orange County Public Schools

The instruction is given to allow the students and teacher
time for exploration, to make mistakes, and then find ways to
recover from those mistakes. This helps them become self-
sufficient in the classroom.

An initial two-and-a-half-hour instructional session cov-
ers the basics of HyperStudio. Each instruction given builds
on the previous instruction. This helps the students to prac-

tice skills so they become automatic. Later the students can concentrate on project content and not the technical aspects of the program.

The speed at which the instruction is given is totally dependent on the class and teacher. Some basic skills need to be in place for a successful session. These include listen and follow verbal instructions; and comprehend and apply the directions left, right, up, down, above, below, inside, and outside. It also helps if the class has some basic computer literacy skills.

The school can prepare for the visit in these ways:

- ♦ Have available one computer loaded with Hyper-Studio for every two students needing instruction. More than two students per computer is not successful. Students do not get enough time to take turns and they become bored with waiting.

- ♦ Have all computers facing the instructor so every screen is seen at the same time. In this way, when verbal instructions are given, the instructor can adjust the speed to the readiness of the group. A television or video display of the computer screen for group viewing is also helpful for some tasks.

- ♦ Pair the students so a good listener is with an exploratory learner. The good listener helps keep the explorer on track and the explorer helps the good listener investigate, make mistakes, and recover from mistakes.

- ♦ If the teacher immediately begins incorporating the use of HyperStudio in the daily classroom routine, the students retain much of the instruction given in the first two-and-a-half-hour session.

Phase Two: Next Steps, Projects, Companion Programs, and Resources

Once a class has created miniprojects using HyperStudio for a few months, a follow-up session is helpful. Additional features of the program are taught and more difficult concepts addressed. As the teacher shows interest, companion products are added. Examples include:

- Helping the teacher learn how to manage student projects with a book containing templates
- Help! I Have HyperStudio: Now What do I Do?
- Management of the created projects, back up files, storage, crashes, and CD-ROM creation
- Introduction to organization and brainstorming
- Places to find photographs on the Internet such as the PhotoShare Collection at http://multimedia. ocps.k12.fl.us/photoshare
- Adding clipart from outside sources such as Flying Colors and KidPix Studio

A variety of follow-up lessons are done for the entire class as demonstrations or for the individual teachers. These include creating AVI/QuickTime movies; creating rolling credits and animations for school news programs; creating projects specifically for the Web; creating videotape portfolios of student work; and teaching the ethical use of others' intellectual property.

Phase Three: Giving Something Back to the Community

The community is defined as any place, group, or organization outside the immediate classroom. Once the teacher has a basic understanding of the concept that they don't have to "know it all" and can be the "facilitator" of student-based multimedia projects, the real world work begins. This concept has been modeled for the teacher in both phases one and two. Phase three sometimes requires that the multimedia instructor and others help the teacher find Giving Something Back projects and leverage for resources so the class can create the projects.

Students and teachers work with other teachers and students, community groups, and nonprofit organizations to create projects. Significant outcomes from this work include teachers changing their instructional style; breaking down barriers between students of different intelligence, ethnic, and skill levels; better working relationships and under-standing between community groups and schools; students observing that their learning has a purpose; and mutual re-spect between teachers and students.

A fifth grade teacher and her class created "software" in the form of HyperStudio stacks for second graders at their school to practice capitalization and the proper use of the word "I." Another fifth grade class created a multimedia mu-seum with a local nonprofit museum in their community. A multiage third/fourth grade class taught all the other fourth graders in their school how to use HyperStudio and created state projects. Several fourth grade classes from different schools created stacks about different endangered species and traded stacks with each other.

Placing the power of multimedia construction in the hands of students and teachers is an exciting endeavor. The variety, sophistication, and type of projects that students and teachers create is truly amazing.

SPECIAL OUTCOMES, RESULTS, AND ACCOMPLISHMENTS

The teachers who exhibit the following behaviors are the most successful workshop participants:

- ◆ A willingness to share what they are learning with others
- ◆ Use of a combination of group instruction and collaborative learning techniques that includes students working as part of a team
- ◆ Good classroom management skills
- ◆ Willingness to learn along with their students
- ◆ Risk takers
- ◆ Staff and faculty members at their work site re-spect them

THINGS TO CONSIDER

Follow-up instruction and visits are key to the success of the models presented. Again, with all the time constraints on teachers, integrating technology into the curriculum can easily be put on the back burner. Supportive administrators who understand the goals of the project are absolutely essential. In some cases, teachers have been moved to another grade level after their initial summer instruction, losing the trained students as part of their program or even changed to a primary grade level for which this project was neither intended nor designed to be used.

COSTS

Total costs are less than $3,000 per team. This includes the purchase of a multimedia computer for each teacher's classroom, HyperStudio, Kaboom!, ClarisWorks, KidPix Studio, and Inspiration; a $50 per day stipend for summer instruction days; substitute pay for follow-up days; and materials printing. The cost does not cover facilities rental or instructor salaries. In the case of the secondary model, some funding can be obtained for salaries in Florida from the state's school funding formula.

CONTACT INFORMATION

Chris Carey
Multimedia Teacher
(407) 317-3200 x2514
e-mail: careyc@ocps.k12.fl.us

Gene Bias
Multimedia Teacher
(407) 317-3200 x2511
e-mail: biasg@ocps.k12.fl.us

TECHNOLOGY PROJECT-BASED SCIENCE

GOALS OF TECHNOLOGY PROGRAM

- To provide conceptual science understandings and experiences through student construction of collaborative, interactive, technology projects
- To integrate student-centered science learning with the development of software simulations

KEYWORDS

- Collaboration
- Multimedia
- Programming
- Project-Based Learning
- Science
- Scientific inquiry

LOCATION

Seeds University Elementary School
UCLA
10636 Circle Drive North
Box 951619
Los Angeles, CA 90095-1619

DESCRIPTION OF SCHOOL AND COMMUNITY

- Nongraded; school is multiage, but essentially Pre-K through 6th
- 480 students and 25 teachers
- School was built in 1947; new addition was added in 1993

- ◆ Students and community are diverse; approximately 21% Hispanic, 14% African American, 10% Asian American, and 41% Caucasian
- ◆ Other factors of interest: constructivist school with faculty members who believe in meeting the needs of a diverse population; curriculum provides instruction with multiple entry points for learners and believes in providing students with multiple ways of knowing and showing what they know; technology is a seamless tool used in every classroom where the computer to student ratio is at least 1:4 and every computer is connected to the Internet

DESCRIPTION OF PROGRAM

Project design features include choice of topics, group collaboration, long-term projects, and artifact production (an interactive technology project, model or simulation made for younger users). When the project begins, students learn the basic LOGO programming concepts of MicroWorlds 2.0 and software design aspects. Students get initial programming practice in teams.

More advanced programming occurs as students need to know. Students ask the teacher, other adults, and peers. They also ask for help online in a MicroWorlds newsgroup, or check the manuals available to learn advanced programming techniques. For example, to show a change in the food supply the student learns to program a "slider" that the user can move in two directions to show an increase or decrease in the food supply.

Second, the topic is introduced. Students generate multiple wonder questions as a group, which they then refine into their personal "driving" questions of inquiry. Students fill out applications for team jobs and are assigned to teams of three to five students. Each team has a computer and adjacent work area where planning boards and materials are available to begin mapping their ideas and timelines for projects. Collaborative team-building activities help students work as an effective team in constructing their projects. Ongoing team-counseling activities provide conflict resolution strategies and help mediate differences in individual student agendas.

Learning activities are large group, small group, and independent. Students may participate in some activities or experiments that the teacher mandates, and may also design their own experiments, investigations, or research. Although this teaching model requires understanding of the topics by the teacher, the teacher also acts as a guide and interpreter of information—not just an information giver. The teacher discusses experiment results, research found on the Internet, and e-mail answers of science experts with each group. The student-centered design and on-demand learning aspects of the projects require flexibility on the part of the teacher.

The project becomes an ongoing cycle of science activities and discussions, science interventions, discussions that link science learning, discussions and refinement of driving questions, advanced programming instruction, and development of collaboratively built SimProjects. (There is simultaneous attention to the main three areas, yet the goal is to link and consistently connect these areas to the others. Ideally, students and teachers are reflecting on how each category connects to the other two categories. Teams are working simultaneously on their personal questions, the science, and the SimProject.)

SPECIAL OUTCOMES, RESULTS, AND ACCOMPLISHMENTS

Students designing software simulations learn about science in a way that demands they connect information meaningfully. When students learn about dolphins, to connect those pieces of information into an ecosystem they must clearly understand the connections and interrelationships. When they explore how temperature, food supply, and number of predators affect animal existence, students must not only understand each of the concepts, but also understand each in relation to the other. They learn about systems in science conceptually. Students go beyond presentation when they are challenged to design and manipulate models that simulate systems of interrelated concepts. When just presenting information, understanding is not really necessary or demonstrated by students. They are simply recalling information they have found or heard. When designing a model, the learning outcomes are different from those in designing presentations. Students formulate and represent their own understanding by manipulating and connecting concepts and relationships in order to construct a model, instead of just telling about the concept. One major difference in project-by-design science is that students are pursuing their research and work on a project during the timeframe of the unit itself. It is not a culmination activity after a science unit. Therefore, as students participate in teacher-directed activities or pursue their own research interests, they are continually applying concepts to the structure of their project. Students must explain how the information or new ideas relate to their project.

THINGS TO CONSIDER

Classroom layout. Computers are in the middle of the room. Students have workstations that include a computer with table space around it for the group to meet and discuss their projects.

Planning Toolbox. Students have a toolbox to build projects. This toolbox includes MicroWorlds, planning boards, calendars, Post-its, software design templates, colored tabs, colored papers, MicroWorlds documentation, MicroWorlds newsgroup, Internet access, books, articles, pictures, expert sources, and teacher/peer guidance.

Science Content. The content of the science program should make connections across the disciplines of life science, earth science, physical science, and space science. However, the distinct concepts and core precepts of these disciplines should also be taught. Teachers need to have a clear understanding of the major concepts they want students to understand by the end of the project. Then, the teacher can provide mandatory and optional activities for students. This program, however, includes the component of on-demand learning. This means that students help decide the course of study for themselves. If students are interested in certain topics, the teacher may provide a clipboard for students to write down their requests. The teacher can then either present whole class lessons and activities, team lessons, or expert group lessons that can be "jigsawed" back to the entire group. On request, teachers may meet with individuals or groups, and help them access expert information via e-mail, telephone, or articles and books.

COSTS

- ◆ Software: multimedia program such as Micro-Worlds or any Logo program
- ◆ Hardware (minimum requirements): seven multimedia computers with Internet access
- ◆ Science supplies for experiments, activities

CONTACT INFORMATION

Cathleen Galas
Demonstration Teacher/Researcher/UES Webmaster
Seeds University Elementary School, UCLA
(310) 825-1801
(310) 206-4452 (Fax)
e-mail: cgalas@ucla.edu

Additional Contact:
Sharon Sutton
Coordinator of Technology and Outreach
Seeds University Elementary School, UCLA
(310) 825-1801
(310) 206-4452 (Fax)
e-mail: ssutton@ucla.edu

http://www-ues.gseis.ucla.edu

TRAIN-THE-TRAINER

GOALS OF TECHNOLOGY PROGRAM

- To enhance and enrich learning opportunities throughout the curriculum
- To increase staff effectiveness and productivity
- To prepare students for lifelong learning and work
- To support and encourage effective creative uses of technology
- To provide instructional technology support and inservice opportunities for faculty

KEYWORDS

- Staff development
- Telecommunication

LOCATION

Redwood High School
395 Doherty Drive
Larkspur, CA 94939

DESCRIPTION OF SCHOOL AND COMMUNITY

- Grades 9–12
- Approximately 1,300 students and 100 teachers
- Facility is 39 years old. Networking began with administration about seven years ago; fiber optics was added four years ago
- Suburban Marin County is 88% Caucasian; Latinos, African Americans, Asians, and Middle Easterners comprise 12%

DESCRIPTION OF PROGRAM

Redwood's technology vision statement is, "Technology is a vital tool to enhance curriculum across all disciplines." The school has almost 200 computers installed in five networked labs (cross-platform computer literacy, PC applications, CAD, science, and open access), the media center, throughout administrative offices, and in most classrooms. Math teachers incorporate graphing calculators, and science teachers use an array of technological learning aids. Staff communication has been enhanced through voicemail and e-mail services. Additionally, broadcasts and news services are available through a video cable download service and a satellite dish connection.

Technological tools have come alive through meaningful applications. Resources include integrated applications, scanning, desktop publishing, multimedia authoring programs, grading applications, scientific computer probes, reference databases, library circulation services, and student-produced WWW pages.

The key to technology incorporation has been faculty direction and support. New faculty are expected to demonstrate computer expertise. Ongoing staff development enables individuals to increase their expertise and ability to incorporate technology into classroom practice. Another important element is the funding of a full-time computer support specialist.

SPECIAL OUTCOMES, RESULTS, AND ACCOMPLISHMENTS

Technology facilitated changes in faculty and staff hiring practices. By embedding technology in the curriculum, many teaching practices have changed.

Every department has explored a variety of technology resources to facilitate student learning and to enhance teacher productivity.

Administrators and counselors use technology to document and assess student work and behavior. This closer supervision has resulted in earlier interventions and more coordinated efforts to help students.

Technology has led to significant enhancements in communications. All faculty and staff members have a new phone/voicemail system and individual voicemail boxes. Most individuals have e-mail and Internet accounts. Also, Redwood High School has installed a sports and events hot-line and anonymous tip hot-line.

The Redwood WWW home page includes daily updates of school bulletins as well as different school features such as an alumni section.

Technology has improved school assessment efforts through computerized records and data analysis to guide decision-making.

DIFFICULTIES (ANTICIPATED AND UNANTICIPATED)

- Financial constraints
- Slow budget process
- Lack of time to install software and hardware
- Lack of teacher knowledge
- Space issues (finding room; the school has grown from 900 to 1300 students in 5 years); computer labs compete for space with classrooms
- Lack of time for teacher training and competing priorities
- Slow time frame for giveing each teacher a class-room computer
- District desire for equitable standards (not have one school ahead of others)

COSTS

Annual Budget:

Equipment upgrades:	$40,000
Repairs:	$10,000
Parent support fund:	$10,000

Software: $5,000–$10,000
Computer specialist: $35,000
Maintenance: $15,000
Startup costs: $75,000 per Lab

CONTACT INFORMATION

Dr. Lesley S. J. Farmer
Library Media Teacher
(415) 945-3663
(415) 945-73675 (Fax)
e-mail: farmer@marin.K12.ca.us

UNIVERSITY HIGH SCHOOL'S WELLNESS ACADEMY

GOALS OF TECHNOLOGY PROGRAM

- To develop an academy that incorporates technology, project-based learning, dual enrollment, and internships to enhance knowledge in the fields of health and wellness
- To expose students to the myriad of career opportunities in the fields of health and wellness
- To equip students with the skills and experience necessary to enter the wellness workforce immediately following high school or to continue their education in wellness at a postsecondary level
- To enhance students' understanding of emerging technologies in the field of wellness

KEYWORDS

- Fitness assessment systems
- Physiology
- Project-based learning
- Wellness

LOCATION

University High School
11550 Lokanotosa Trail
Orlando, FL 32817

DESCRIPTION OF SCHOOL AND COMMUNITY

University High School is located in Orlando, Florida near the University of Central Florida. The school encompasses 95 acres and houses over 180 classrooms. The high school has grades 9–12 and a total enrollment of approximately 3,700 students. About 90 students are members of the Wellness Academy. The Wellness Academy staff consists of ten teachers including strength specialists, exercise physiologists, nutritionists, technological support staff, and wellness experts. The Academy was established in 1997 and is consistently in a state of growth, looking for the most up-to-date technology, equipment, and ideas to enhance programs.

DESCRIPTION OF PROGRAM

The University Wellness Academy offers a specialized field of study that can be elected by the student. Students must go through an application process and must be accepted into the Academy before they can begin their curriculum of study. The mission is to promote the academic, physical, and social development of students as they explore careers in the fields of health and wellness. In an attempt to reach these goals, instructors incorporate technology, internships, dual enrollment, and project-based learning.

Technology

The TriFit 600 Fitness Assessment System is the most technologically advanced fitness assessment program available. It is designed to test a person's body composition, strength, flexibility, cardiovascular integrity, and blood pressure. As a result of this testing, the TriFit 600 can assist in putting a student on a specialized exercise and diet program. At the conclusion of this test, it gives a detailed printout of the fitness level of the person. All of the members of the Wellness Academy are trained in the use of this equipment. They are also well-versed in analyzing the results of the Trifit test, as well as developing personalized programs for each client based on the results of the test.

The Futrex 5000 is a body fat analysis computer that uses infrared light to estimate body fat percentage. The Futrex then gives a detailed printout of the person's level of fitness. This computer is compact and can be carried in a small briefcase. The portability of the Futrex system allows the teachers and students from the Academy to take fitness technology into the community.

The University Wellness Academy also uses CSI Fitness Assessment Software. This computer program can be used by large groups of students. The students enter the results of a multitude of tests, which the system analyzes and then gives the students a basic fitness profile. The students' records are kept on file for the four years they are in the wellness program; this allows the academy to monitor the students' progress over the four years.

The University Wellness Academy also uses a program called Power. This computer program allows users to develop personalized exercise and weight-training programs based on the results of several different tests. It sets up specialized programs for individuals in their particular sports. Training regimens are formulated for each athlete's ability. This program has the ability to create specialized workouts to maximize athletic performance. The routines vary as the athlete moves in and out of season.

In addition to using the TriFit and Futrex equipment, and the Power and CSI software, the University Wellness Academy has a wide variety of fitness equipment that incorporates technology. It uses Polar Heart Rate monitors with students to check heart rates while exercising. These monitors are worn around the chest along with an additional piece worn on the wrist. The piece on the chest sends a signal to the wrist piece that allows students to simply look at their wrist to monitor their heart rate. This is tremendously beneficial to the curriculum when attempting to teach the students concepts such as resting heart rate and target heart rate. The Academy has stationary bikes, stair steppers, rowers, and treadmills that all have computers to monitor speed, calories burned, revolutions per minute, and so forth. The Academy's most state-of-the-art piece of fitness equipment is the Quinton Heartrate Plus Treadmill. This equipment actually has specialized programs that students can choose while exercising. This wide variety of equipment allows teachers to incorporate technology into the program even while students are exercising.

Internships

The University Wellness Academy plans to offer a wide range of internships in a variety of different settings such as wellness centers, rehabilitation facilities, orthopedic offices, hospitals, and health clubs. This experience gives students an opportunity to facilitate their learning in a real-world setting, as well as to work with professionals in a most technologically advanced setting. Students gain entry into the expanding field of wellness before they graduate from high school.

Project-Based Learning

The University Wellness Academy emphasizes a program centered on project-based learning. Students work with "clients" on an individual basis. They establish individualized programs for their clients as well as monitor their clients' progress with the use of the technological resources available. This allows the students to take ownership of their responsibilities.

SPECIAL OUTCOMES, RESULTS, AND ACCOMPLISHMENTS

The University High School Wellness Academy has one major goal: to promote the academic, physical, and social development of its students as they explore the fields of health and wellness. However, in working toward this goal, faculty have accomplished much more than planned. First, as a result of the implementation of this program the fitness level of both students and many faculty and staff has improved. Second, the school has received a tremendous amount of support and involvement from the community. Last, the students take more responsibility for their assignments, projects, and clients. The biggest change is the heightened awareness of fitness and overall health on the campus.

In addition to the improved understanding of fitness, staff members have established important links with the community.

Wellness facilities in the immediate area offer internships, field trips, special training, and a multitude of other benefits. Working with the community allows students to experience real-world applications in the workplace. In essence, affiliations with the community enable students to apply their knowledge of wellness through on-the-job experience.

These aspects of the program allows participants to deviate from the norm. It allows the school to give back to the community, as opposed to needing help from the community. One of the services the school offers is fitness testing and assessments for community groups (e.g., Rotary Clubs, private industries, other educational facilities). This allows the Academy to be an integral part of community building, instead of being a community byproduct.

The most impressive outcome of student learning is a heightened level of responsibility. This is a problem on almost any level of schooling. Some students simply do not care whether they succeed or fail. Academy students have begun to show a genuine interest in the success of the program, as well as in the success of their clients.

DIFFICULTIES (ANTICIPATED AND UNANTICIPATED)

One of the difficulties the Academy has encountered is trying to distinguish the program from a traditional physical education program. The PE program is a separate entity from the wellness program. The two are closely related, but the University Wellness Academy is the study of the components of health and wellness. The University High School PE program centers on the skill-related aspects of sports. Both are vital to the education of the students, but there must be a distinction between the two.

A second difficulty is trying to keep up with the technology. The program is growing so quickly, that many of the technological systems are utilized to the point where multiple systems are needed. For example, the TriFit 600 system is the most vital piece of equipment in use; however, it is almost at the point where one system is not enough to handle the number of users.

COSTS

Weight Room Facilities $100,000
    East Campus Weight Room
    West Campus Weight Room
    Olympic Lifting Room
Cardiovascular Facility $40,000
Software $16,500

CONTACT INFORMATION

Judy Cunningham, Principal
Kimrey Ross-Myers, School of Human Services Coordinator
Jeff Boettner, Dean of Students
Cindy Boettner, Wellness Academy Curriculum Leader
Mike Weems, Exercise Physiologist
University High School Wellness Academy
11550 Lokanotosa Trail
Orlando, FL 32817
(407) 275-7627

USING MULTIMEDIA TO CREATE A CUSTOM CD-ROM ENCYCLOPEDIA

GOALS OF TECHNOLOGY PROGRAM

- To create a multimedia custom CD-ROM encyclopedia of African Americans who are natives of the community and who have made local, state, and national contributions to the country
- To increase parental and community involvement in the educational process of students
- To ensure successful, effective, and efficient use of technologies beyond the traditional classroom hardware
- To promote the rich history of the county
- To provide positive and memorable educational experiences for students
- To refine and advance computer skill of both teachers and students

KEYWORDS

- History
- Multimedia

LOCATION

Stewart Street Elementary School
749 South Stewart Street
Quincy, FL 32351

DESCRIPTION OF SCHOOL AND COMMUNITY

- Grades Pre-K–5
- Approximately 850 students

- Facility is approximately 32 years old
- Stewart Street Elementary is located 22 miles west of Tallahassee in a rural town
- The student population is approximately 3% are Caucasian, 94% African American, and 3% Hispanic

DESCRIPTION OF PROGRAM

Preparing students to produce a product of this magnitude was a challenge and a learning experience, and rewarding. Development of an electronic encyclopedia involved both parents and community participation. Gadsden County, Florida is a rural community where the majority population is African American. The teacher wanted to increase student awareness of the historical contributions made on the local, state, and national levels by natives of their hometown.

A time line was created to help students meet deadlines. Students checked time lines daily to stay on track. Also, a wall chart was erected for students to check-off completed assignments. Students recorded their progress in a journal throughout the project. As a recipient of a $250,000 grant, shared among five schools, the school was able to purchase hardware plus auxiliary equipment, which included a 5300 Power Mac AV computer, digital camera, Quick Cam and Powerbook. Software purchases were Writing Center, Avidvideoshop, and HyperStudio. Planning and being knowledgeable in different applications and in the use of different hardware was an important component for continued success. The art teacher, in a joint effort, provided training in Photoshop and in the use of a scanner. The school did not solicit outside sources for training students.

Students viewed Compton and Grolier electronic encyclopedias to observe how backgrounds, categories, borders, quicktime movies, biographies, text, and quizzes could enhance the project. After viewing the electronic encyclopedias they had a more concrete idea of the outcome of the final product to be created with HyperStudio.

To select participants for the project letters were mailed with a detailed descriptive form about the importance of the project and to solicit their participation. A biographical sketch and a photo were requested on the descriptive form. Meanwhile, students were working on interview techniques, courtesy skills, and professionalism, which was invaluable to success of the project. The teachers were not present when students greeted and interviewed particpants. Of course, when students interviewed a celebrity they felt overwhelmed, so they began to keep an autograph book. Students were assigned these specific jobs:

- Authors—students wrote, typed, and created quizzes pertaining to each person's life
- Videographers—students were trained in the utilization and operation of a video camera
- Interviewers—students interviewed each person with a list of prearranged questions in school's television station
- Scanners—students scanned all photos and articles, and copied them onto diskette
- Video editors—students edited video clippings from interview tapes and made a quick time movie; if no photo was submitted, a still shot was taken from video clipping and the selection of different transitions allowed for a smoother move from question to question
- Technicians—students connected and disconnected to and from auxiliary equipment
- Designers and graphic artists—students imported and edited background and clipart

All students were required to master at least two different jobs and every one had to skillfully connect and disconnect hardware to and from auxiliary equipment. Four different computers were used to store data. One computer was dedicated to video editing, and another was used to design stacks. LCIIs stored authors' work, and the computer connected to the scanner was used solely for editing photos and articles. All photos, biographies, and background cards were transferred to the computer where quicktime movies were located.

The encyclopedia categories were *Education, Sports, Businesses, Politics, Civil Rights, Women in Politics, Organizations, Arts,* and *First.* Each category was designed with a cover card that linked to an individual in that particular category. All cards linked backed to an index with all persons listed alphabetically. The index card was created to easily locate individuals. Due to the maturity level of the 5th graders, the teacher used a password to lock all stacks after editing. The project was pressed on recordable CD's. A label and cover was designed to reflect the subject and school.

SPECIAL OUTCOMES, RESULTS, AND ACCOMPLISHMENTS

- Students became knowledgeable in the operation of media hardware used to develop and deliver presentations
- Students' technical and troubleshooting skills increased
- Because of their expertise, students have assisted in several computer training programs for teachers
- Students learned nontraditional research methods while sharpening their written and oral language skills
- Students were guest speakers at the opening session of the 1997 Florida Education Technology Conference (FETC) where they made history as the first group of Florida students to serve as presenters at FETC
- Students have become pioneers in the educational system of Gadsden County
- Students have preserved a portion of the African American history of their hometown

DIFFICULTIES (ANTICIPATED AND UNANTICIPATED)

It took a great deal of afterhours work to train students in video-editing software, Photoshop, and interviewing techniques. Also, participants selected for the project needed time to gather photos and other information pertaining to their accomplishments. Working towards a deadline was most important.

THINGS TO CONSIDER

- ♦ Maturity level of students to be trained
- ♦ Retrieval and storage problems
- ♦ Copyright issues
- ♦ Selection of persons or organizations to be honored

COSTS

Project expenses were supported by a $50,000 grant.

CONTACT INFORMATION

Estelle Price
850-627-6030
e-mail: pricee@mail.firn.edu

USING TECHNOLOGY TO INCREASE DELIVERY OF COURSES TO RURAL STUDENTS

GOALS OF TECHNOLOGY PROGRAM

- ◆ To offer high quality courses to rural students in a poor district in order to allow them to overcome the limitations of the isolated environment
- ◆ To have students use a variety of technological tools in learning activities
- ◆ To increase the independence of students in taking charge of their own learning

KEYWORDS

- ◆ Individualized education
- ◆ Multimedia
- ◆ Rural education

LOCATION

Ackerman High School and Weir Attendance Center
Choctaw County School District
Box 398, 126 East Quinn
Ackerman, MS 39735

DESCRIPTION OF SCHOOL AND COMMUNITY

- ◆ Grades 7–12 in Ackerman High School and grades K–12 in Weir Attendance Center
- ◆ Ackerman High School has about 500 students, and Weir Attendance Center has about 600 students; each school has about 40 teachers
- ◆ Ackerman High School is approximately 55 years old, but was renovated in 1994 after a fire. The

oldest part of Weir Attendance Center is approximately 50 years old

♦ Choctaw County School District is in Choctaw County, Mississippi. It is approximately 100 miles north of Jackson. There are approximately 8,500 people in the county and 1,900 students in the district. The two high schools are Ackerman High School and Weir Attendance Center. Ackerman's student population is approximately 35% African American and 65% Caucasian. Weir's student population is approximately 50% African American and 50% Caucasian. About 70% of students are on free or reduced-cost lunches

♦ All classrooms in both schools have network connections with access to the Internet, but not all classrooms have computers

DESCRIPTION OF PROGRAM

This program is designed so that one teacher with a liberal arts background, who is capable of using available technology, can teach students in two rural high schools subjects that are not taught in the regular classroom but that are needed in preparation for college. The program has constantly evolved through its 16 years, but it has always involved the use of computers and other technology. Students learn the subject they are taking, work independently, and use modern technology to learn and to do their assignments.

Students learn to work independently because the courses are taught, or facilitated, in an independent learning environment using both individual and small group instruction. The teacher is at each school for three periods during the day, and there is an aide who stays at each school throughout the day. The program offers courses that are facilitated by the teacher and courses that are delivered through distance learning. If students are taking a teacher-facilitated course, they are assigned to the program while the teacher is in the school. If they are taking distance-learning courses, they are assigned during whatever time the course is offered. The teacher-facilitated courses include physics, anatomy and physiology, astronomy, environmental science, marine biology, calculus, mythology, humanities, creative writing, French, German, and various computer courses. The teacher is presently certified by the state to teach these courses. The distance-learning courses that have been offered include Latin, Spanish, Russian, Japanese, advanced English, world geography, and art. If possible, courses are added on student request.

Students in the program use modern technology to learn and to do their assignments. Many courses involve active student research using CD-ROMs and the Internet, in addition to print materials, and student presentation of the research using word processors and presentation or multimedia software. Students in French and German also use a teacher-written vocabulary drill program, audiotapes, videotapes, satellite broadcasts in the target language, and CD-ROMs. Students may research a town or area in the country they are studying and then make a multimedia presentation of their results using HyperStudio. Mythology and humanities students research topics and then use word processors or multimedia authoring programs to present their work. They are beginning to use Knowledge Forum from Learning in Motion to allow them to work collaboratively across the WAN of the district so that students taking these subjects in both schools and during any period can work together in constructing knowledge on a topic.

Students in science courses make use of computer-based laboratory equipment and videodiscs, as well as more traditional experiment equipment and procedures. They have also used a simulation program in which they design and implement their own simulations, and they have used image processing software. Physics students are presently using the Comprehensive Conceptual Curriculum for Physics (C3P) from the University of Dallas. They use calculator-based laboratory interfaces and Science Workshop from Pasco with basic mechanics and optics equipment to perform experiments and then use spreadsheets and computer generated graphs to present their work. Extra projects include student-made simulations of physics topics such as a projectile or a sled going down a hill using VisSim or Interactive Physics and investigations of pictures from space with Hands on Image Processing (HIP) Physics from the University of Arizona. Anatomy and Physiology students work with the A.D.A.M. anatomy software and also with the physiology units. They study histology with Videodiscovery's Anatomy and Physiology videodisc. They study control systems through the use of an activity on the renal system developed in the Frontiers Science Teacher Summer Research Program. Students use HIP Biology to study MRIs and CAT scans, and VisSim to stimulate a concept such as the control systems found in the kidney. Environmental science students research the various biomes and the plants and animals found in each. They then make a HyperStudio stack showing their research. They use JEDI discs from the US Geological Survey to study the effects of melting polar ice on land masses.

SPECIAL OUTCOMES, RESULTS, AND ACCOMPLISHMENTS

The program began with one teacher as a federally funded experimental program in Ackerman High School. The district concluded that the program was a success and decided to make it available in both high schools.

With the addition of distance learning to the program, an aide was added at each school to make the program available when the teacher was at the other school.

In the first years of the program, student ACT scores for the district increased markedly. ACT scores of students who complete courses in the program remain higher than those of the students who do not take courses in the program.

Students learn to work collaboratively to complete projects.

Many students in the program have also participated in academic competitions and are now members of the county academic teams.

DIFFICULTIES (ANTICIPATED AND UNANTICIPATED)

♦ Some students find it difficult to work independently

♦ The teacher must attend conferences and search constantly for new practices in order to stay current in the use of technology

THINGS TO CONSIDER

♦ Buy the hardware needed to run the software that best carries out the educational objectives

♦ Keeping current with technology can be expensive, but in many cases, older technology remains useful and can expand the total technology inventory

♦ Because students work individually or in small groups and because the teacher teaches in two schools, the total amount of technology needed is smaller than if buying for several classrooms and teachers

♦ This program should begin small but grow larger as the teacher feels more comfortable

COSTS

Startup costs for one school:

Hardware:	$10,000
Software:	$5,000
Science equipment:	$3,000
Videodisc player and discs:	$2,000
TV, VCR, and videos:	$2,000
Optional distance learning (satellite):	$5,000

Operational costs

New hardware:	$2,000
Supplies:	$2,000
Conferences/training for teacher:	$1,000

CONTACT INFORMATION

Dr. Frances Coleman
Teacher and District Technology Coordinator
(601) 285-3667 or 601-547-6880
(601) 285-3815 (Fax)
e-mail: fcoleman@mail.telapex.com

VIDEO CONFERENCING FOR COLLABORATIVE LEARNING

GOALS OF TECHNOLOGY PROGRAM

- To involve students in collaborative learning with students in other locations through video conferencing
- To help students develop better communication skills
- To engage students in higher-level thinking

KEYWORDS

- Communications
- Cooperative learning
- Multicultural education
- Science
- Video

LOCATION

Ithaca City School District
400 Lake Street
Ithaca, NY 14851

DESCRIPTION OF SCHOOL AND COMMUNITY

- 6,000 students and 570 teachers in district
- 12 schools in district including 8 elementary schools, 2 middle schools, 1 high school, and an alternative 6–12 school
- The district includes urban, suburban, and rural populations

Description of Program

Numerous classes in the district have participated in video conferencing learning activities. In video conferencing, a class can see and hear another class in real-time from a distant location. For video conferencing, the schools use their Internet connection, a PowerMac or Pentium computer, a Quickcam, and White Pine's Enhanced CuSeeMe software (the video conferencing software). Video conferencing allows students to collaborate with other students in interactive learning experiences.

In one application, they created a "Tree" video conference with one of the local first grade classes and a middle school in Renton, Washington. After the teachers introduced their classes, a group of students from the first grade class told the Renton students about a local tree and showed them pictures of the tree. After the group finished, they asked Renton if they had the same tree and listened for their response. This pattern continued for each of the first grade groups. A chart was created to show the similarities and differences in the trees in each location. Then, the Renton group told about its trees, showed pictures, and asked if those trees existed in the first graders' area.

In another video conference, a sixth grade class participated in a science observation with a kindergarten class. The kindergarten class gave five clues to the sixth graders who, in groups, tried to figure out the object. When they could not identify it, they asked for more clues. The kindergarten students happily stumped the older students with clues such as "It is dry. It is round. It has lines. It is flat. It is wet." The sixth graders felt no object could have "contradictory" properties, but a pumpkin does! The sixth graders were infuriated when the kindergartners guessed their object with the first five clues. They wanted a rematch.

An especially interesting video conference involved fourth graders who video conferenced with a class in Paris, France about their schools. The American students were very surprised that these French students did not match their mental image of French students. They discovered that certain words such as "old" can have different meanings. After a group told about their school day, the other group compared it to their day. The American students enjoyed learning about French school life and especially enjoyed singing a song together in French.

SPECIAL OUTCOMES, RESULTS, AND ACCOMPLISHMENTS

Students learn many skills when they video conference. They learn a tremendous amount of content and much cultural information. They learn how important it is to speak clearly and loudly. They learn that their body communicates much information. The students realize that they learn from visuals as well as sound. They discover that they can learn from other students in other locations. They like that they can personally interact in real-time with other students.

DIFFICULTIES (ANTICIPATED AND UNANTICIPATED)

There are many technological difficulties (e.g., working reflector, network problems, software conflicts; slow perframe rate; adequate but not terrific sound). The physical location of other schools (the French school for example) can create a major time difference. Students need to practice their presentations, have effective visuals, and know how to move quietly so as not to disturb other presenters.

COSTS

Pentium or Power Mac:	$1,500
Quickcam and software:	$100
White Pine Enhanced CuSeeMe:	$100
Fast network (not dial-in)	

CONTACT INFORMATION

Harry Tuttle
Technology Integration Teacher
607-272-4493
607-272-4493 (Fax)
e-mail: harryt3@aol.com

WAKELAND ELEMENTARY'S TECHNOLOGY—HOME CONNECTION

GOALS OF TECHNOLOGY PROGRAM

- ◆ To foster a positive home-school relationship with the parents of the participating at-risk students
- ◆ To create a technology home-school connection with the technology software and hardware needed to improve basic skills and that will positively motivate the at-risk students

KEYWORDS

At-risk students
Parent Involvement

LOCATION

Wakeland Elementary School
Manatee County
1812-27th Street East
Bradenton, FL 34208

DESCRIPTION OF SCHOOL AND COMMUNITY

- ◆ Grades Pre-K–5
- ◆ Approximately 680 students and 47 teachers
- ◆ Facility is 25 years old (recently renovated)
- ◆ Wakeland Elementary School is located in Bradenton, Florida. The area's major industries are agriculture, tourism, with some technology and manufacturing firms

DESCRIPTION OF PROGRAM

Wakeland Elementary's Technology—Home Connection was developed as an outreach to the community as a direct result of a needs assessment focusing on utilizing technology for the students combined with a stockpile of Apple IIe computers tha were sitting idle after the implementation of a school technology retrofit project. Fifth grade students were recommended for the program by their teachers. To be "eligible" to receive a computer, a student had to show a high level of responsibility and respect for property. Parents had to show responsibility by being involved in the school life of their child (by attending the county-mandated report card pickup conference, being a member of the PTO, and/or by creating a responsible environment for their child by the simple act of ensuring that homework assignments were completed). Once recommended, student names were submitted to the technology team and a prioritized list was made. Families were notified and requested to complete a response form. The responses were sent back in record time. Some students actually ran back to school with the completed slips on the same day the slips were sent home! To quote the letter to parents, "…it is quite an honor to have been chosen to participate in this partnership. It is our wish that this program will help keep the bond strong between home and school. We also know that you will enjoy getting your hands on this technology and sharing it with your family."

The students were given hands-on training that included setting up the unit that was assigned to them and sampling the MECC instructional software programs that were available for checkout. Four MECC programs were sent home with the computer in a large envelope with instructions on the basic operation of the Apple IIe computer. The MECC programs are exchanged once a week on an as-needed basis. The students use the computers to reinforce the basic skills taught at school by using the MECC programs. The popular programs are Number Munchers, Letter Munchers, and the tried but true Oregon Trail. Speedway Math and Fraction Munchers are sometimes assigned by the participant's teachers as review for students. There is an Apple IIe set up at school with a dot matrix printer in case the student needs to print anything from AppleWorks. The student just brings the 5.25 disk to school and prints from the disk.

The outcomes of this project far exceeded any expectations of the staff at Wakeland. The parents have responded with heart-warming comments such as, "...having the computer in our home is the best thing that has happened to my child. We don't even turn on the television!" One parent came to school with tear-filled eyes thanking the teacher and expressing the gratitude felt by the family "for believing in us."

SPECIAL OUTCOMES, RESULTS, AND ACCOMPLISHMENTS

The students are highly motivated to "qualify" for this program. This is also true for the parents! Teachers report that the parents of the students in this program are more likely to show at the first conference! After the first year of implementation, the students completed a survey and rated the program as something to continue throughout the school year for more students throughout the school.

DIFFICULTIES (ANTICIPATED AND UNANTICIPATED)

The most difficult part of the program was to choose the students to leave out. As word of this program spread around the school, teachers found that the students were highly motivated to participate, so the school had to limit the participants to the number of computers. The school is considering advertising on the Internet to have "richer" schools share the wealth of their older computers so that more students will be able to participate in this wonderful opportunity.

THINGS TO CONSIDER

The students need to have a room to use for training and turning in the equipment. This takes up a lot of space and it requires heavy lifting. The school is space-challenged and had to close its computer lab during the checkout time.

COSTS

The only costs were in the purchase of envelopes (for the diskettes and directions), printing, and some video cables. So far there have been no costs associated with maintenance of the computers.

CONTACT INFORMATION

Ellen R. Lopez
Instructional Technology Coordinator
(941) 741-3518
(941) 741-3549 (Fax)
e-mail: lopeze89@bhip.infi.net

WINONA MIDDLE SCHOOL MEDIA PROGRAM

GOALS OF TECHNOLOGY PROGRAM

- To provide materials, instruction, and services that meet the curricular, recreational, and information literacy needs of middle-level learners
- To complement the middle school philosophy of providing an active, exploratory learning environment that meets the needs of middle-level learners
- To work with faculty through the curriculum development process to integrate media and technology into all curriculum areas
- To address Minnesota Graduation Standards
- To provide staff development experiences that help educators become effective and efficient users of technology for instruction and instructional management
- To serve as a model program for preservice teachers at higher education institutions in the community
- To provide leadership, services, and information to other building media programs and to district programs as needed

KEYWORDS

- Curriculum integration
- Cooperative learning
- Preservice education
- Staff development

LOCATION

Winona Middle School
ISD 861
166 West Broadway
Winona, MN 55987

DESCRIPTION OF SCHOOL AND COMMUNITY

- ◆ Grades 6–8
- ◆ Approximately 1,100 students and 80 teachers
- ◆ Buildings are 80–90 years old
- ◆ Population is primarily lower-middle to upper-middle class Caucasian; small minority of African American, Hmong, and other Asian groups
- ◆ Winona is a rural community of 25,000 located on the Mississippi River in extreme southeast Minnesota. The economy is a mix of high technology, low-tech manufacturing, and higher education. A relatively high percentage of the population has Internet access. There are three postsecondary institutions in the community and several private schools. Tourism is becoming increasingly important in southeast Minnesota

DESCRIPTION OF PROGRAM

The Winona Middle School Media Program is a strong, highly integrated program that provides all media and technology services to the school. The high degree of curricular integration has been achieved through vision, staff development, strong administrative support, staff support, and the curriculum writing and planning process.

Most classrooms are connected to the schoolwide Ethernet network, as are four of the school's five computer labs. An Ethernet network provides access to online resources in the media center and at other locations. Some of the networked resources in the technology-rich school are T1 Internet access; Computer Cat/Matter of Fact; Discover Career Resources; Middle Search; Biology Digest; UXL Biographies; The World

Book Multimedia Encyclopedia; and The Gale-Net DISCovering Resources. The presence of extensive technology has not diminished the print collection and circulation of print resources continues to increase.

Most classroom computers are Power Macs. In keeping with the philosophy of rewarding the power users, teachers who attend staff development classes and integrate technology heavily in their curriculum are among those who receive upgrades as new computers are purchased. Many teachers are implementing paperless projects and students often participate in multiple projects at any one time.

Additional media center secretarial staff were hired as the school acquired more technology; parent volunteers help extend media center hours beyond the school day. The Media Center is also used in community education projects and by the local ISP provider when the provider offers training.

The school's Web site was originally designed for Winona Middle School by US WEST Advanced Technologies when US WEST worked with the Luminet, a community video and data network. Since then, the school media specialist and district network specialist have maintained the popular site. Of special value are sections on eight ethnic groups that settled in Winona and a collection of staff development handouts.

Staff development is a major component of the media and technology programs. Most classes are offered after school and provide continuing education incentives for staff. The current emphasis is toward offering classes that help staff use technology as they implement Minnesota Graduation Standard Performance packages that address inquiry and technology. This means moving beyond the introductory and skill level classes into integration-level classes such as "Searching Electronically," "Designing Lessons that Integrate Technology," and "Internet Search Engines." Daytime opportunities provide teachers with extended blocks of time to work in the media center to explore resources, develop lessons and plan with the media specialist. New teachers are especially encouraged to take advantage of this opportunity. The results of the strong staff development program are apparent as teachers are well-prepared to provide technology- based opportunities for their students.

The Middle School media specialist chairs "Celebrating Success with Technology," the annual four-day district summer technology academy for teachers. The academy is well attended by district staff as well as staff from neighboring school districts. The academy's goals are to increase staff technology skills and ability to integrate technology into the curriculum. Additional information about technology staff development and handouts from classes are available on the school's Web site: http://wms.luminet.net/wmstechnology/index.html. All classes are taught by district teachers, providing them an opportunity to learn from their peers and to share ideas. The district staff development committee funds the academy and there is no cost to district teachers. Staff members from area schools pay a small fee, and the 1997 income was used to provide blocks of time for up to 45 teachers from throughout the district to work with their building media specialist and resources.

Curricular integration of technology is high and all students have multiple and extended opportunities to use technology. Usage is especially high in the traditional core subjects such as science and social studies, but computer and information technology are used heavily in math, health, music, and industrial technology. Geography projects have evolved from reports into multiple, multimedia, and sometimes paperless-based projects completed at all grade levels. Sixth and eighth grade science students have completed extensive inquiry-based projects in which they use resources in all formats to answer a question. Scheduling the media center and labs is competitive with facilities often scheduled weeks and months in advance. The school has found that projects extended over a period of time rather than those implemented over a two to three-day period are the most successful. A longer time period gives students time to reflect on their instruction. Use of technology is seamless as students routinely use technology to access and communicate information.

Budgets have remained strong and are a considerable portion of the school's budget. PTA support and some grants have helped provide some additional funding for technology.

Located only two blocks from Winona State University, the media program also provides opportunities for pre-service teachers to have first-hand experience working with students and technology.

SPECIAL OUTCOMES, RESULTS, AND ACCOMPLISHMENTS

- The media/technology program is highly recognized, valued, and regarded in the school district and community. It is a frequent site of visits by personnel from other school districts
- Parents expect their students to have access to information and contribute to the program through volunteer efforts
- Winona Middle School received the 1997 Information Technology Award from Multimedia Schools and Gale Research
- The media specialist and the principal have each won state awards from the Minnesota Educational Media Organization (MEMO)
- The school's Web site is often cited as a good site
- The program has been a beta site for Winnebago Software and World Book products

DIFFICULTIES (ANTICIPATED AND UNANTICIPATED)

In October 1996, the voters of District 861 approved a new Middle School. Staff members now face the new challenge of planning facilities and a delivery system to meet the needs of the 21st century.

THINGS TO CONSIDER

The success of the program is an example of how vision and desire can go a long way. Old facilities and the necessity of purchasing technology slowly have never been a deterrent. The program was thriving long before the advent of the Ethernet network, T1 Internet connectivity, and districtwide funding for technology began in 1995.

COSTS

The building budget averages $30,000 per year. Each year the media center also receives $5,000 from the business office to be used as needed; traditionally, it is used to buy additional technology. The district technology budget and PTA contributions also provide funding.

CONTACT INFORMATION

Mary Alice Anderson
Media Specialist
(507) 454-9439
(507) 454-9436 (Fax)
e-mail: maryalice@wms.luminet.net
Media Specialist's WWW page: http://wms.luminet.net/
   teachers/manderso.html
School WWW site: http://wms.luminet.net

WOW—T 'N' T
WINDOWS ONLINE TO THE WORLD—
THEN 'N' TODAY ONLINE
INTERGENERATIONAL LIVING HISTORY

GOALS OF TECHNOLOGY PROGRAM

+ To empower students to embark on an online learning adventure
+ To exchange traditional social studies books for an exciting intergenerational, "telecollaborative," online, entry-level Internet living history experience
+ To guide students in the development of telecommunication skills through "real research" online and desktop publishing skills while "writing for real reasons"

KEYWORDS

+ Cooperative learning
+ Desktop publishing
+ Internet
+ Senior citizens
+ Telecommunications

LOCATION

Eatontown Public Schools
Meadowbrook School
Wyckoff Road
Eatontown, NJ 07724

DESCRIPTION OF SCHOOL AND COMMUNITY

+ Grades K–6
+ Approximately 480 students and 30 teachers

♦ Facility is approximately 30 years old and is located in Eatontown, New Jersey next to Fort Monmouth, a military installation. The area supports many electronic industries and shopping malls. Caucasian, African American, Hispanic, and Asian families live in the community

DESCRIPTION OF PROGRAM

The Online Intergenerational Living History program has proven to be an exciting interview project that provided a practical, realistic, easy to replicate, entry-level Internet experience for K-6 students. Senior citizen keypals' personalizing of history, through their remembrances of their experiences during the twentieth century, has made historical facts come alive for students.

Meadowbrook School's fourth grade students and a group of senior citizen HOSTS (Help One Student To Succeed) mentors, working in the SCAN (Senior Citizen Activity Center) computer lab at Monmouth Mall, have formed a pilot learning partnership to bridge the generations. By communicating online, they shared questions and answers about life during the twentieth century when these senior citizen keypals were growing up.

Cooperative learning groups of students did online research and composed e-mail questions on their classroom computers using ClarisWorks. They saved their messages to their senior citizen keypals on disk so that their questions could be copied and pasted into the e-mail form on a computer that was online. (See the examples on pages 253 and 254.)

Senior citizen keypals, students, parents, teachers, and administrators have all enthusiastically endorsed this project. They have found it to be a meaningful and stimulating method of learning history, developing telecommunication and desktop publishing skills, and improving cooperative learning skills.

WOW / Transportation

Hi Mrs. Johnson,

1. What kind of car did you drive? What color was it? Did you like driving in it?

2. Did you ever ride in a blimp? If so, what was it like?

3. Did you ever go on a cruise? If so, explain what it was like.

4. Did you ever ride on a steam boat? If so, what was it like?

Christina, Kelli, Jennifer, Gregory

To: MDBK School
Subj: Transportation/Kelli's Group
Greetings Christina, Kelli, Jennifer, Gregory

I'm looking forward to exchanging information with you during the next few weeks. I don't have answers for all of your questions, but I'll do my best.

1. My dad had a black Buick which he drove when I was growing up. He took us to school in it every morning. I remember rolling the windows down on hot days because cars didn't have air conditioning then. I didn't own my own car until after I graduated from college and started going to work. That car was a blue Plymouth, and I was about the fourth person to own it. New cars were too expensive to buy!

2. I never rode in a blimp because the last passenger blimp, the Hindenburg, blew up before I was born.

3. Going on a cruise is one of my favorite vacations. My first cruises were to Bermuda and Nassau. The best cruise I went on was in Europe on the Mediterranean. I left from Greece and visited several islands on the way to Turkey. After that we travelled to Istanbul, a city which has one half in Europe and one half in Asia. (If you get a chance, see if you can find it on a world map.) We travelled at night so that each day we were in a new port where we could go sightseeing. We also ate LOTS of food.

4. Sorry, I haven't ever had a chance to ride on a steam boat.

I'll be waiting for your next set of questions. Good luck with your project.

Mrs. Johnson

SPECIAL OUTCOMES, RESULTS, AND ACCOMPLISHMENTS

Meeting in their cooperative learning groups to compose well–thought-out questions for their senior citizen keypals, students discovered that they needed to do some "real research" through a variety of sources (books, CD-ROMS, Internet, etc.). By "writing for real reasons," students were given opportunities to improve their communication skills while they explored the Internet through this guided curriculum-related project and published their findings on their computers.

The format of this project provided the flexibility needed to overcome the coordination problems of accessing and using the Internet with K–6 students during school hours.

Internet security concerns were easily handled. Incoming e-mail messages to students were screened by teachers for appropriateness of message content before students read and printed them to share with their classmates. At the end of the school year these living history accounts were published as a looseleaf notebook of e-mail.

To review and share the historical information compiled during this project, game cards were made on the computer for an intergenerational "What Do You Know About Life in the 20th Century?" BINGO game.

DIFFICULTIES (ANTICIPATED AND UNANTICIPATED)

Because of the popularity of computer classes at the Monmouth Mall SCAN computer lab, senior citizen keypals sometimes had difficulty sending their e-mail. Some senior keypals also went to Florida for the winter. Consequently, some keypals sent their e-mail from their home computers in New Jersey or in Florida.

THINGS TO CONSIDER

A project coordinator is needed to help teachers establish guidelines to enhance students and senior citizen keypals opportunities for success.

Teachers must meet and compile materials to teach students interviewing skills and to set up a cooperative learning plan.

Time must be scheduled for weekly research and writing of e-mail from each group of students to their online senior citizen keypals.

Each day a different student was chosen to monitor his or her classmates' e-mail composing, editing, and saving on a disk. This student became a facilitator for other students, enabling the teacher to continue uninterrupted classroom work. Most importantly, students practiced technology and editing skills, while increasing their self-esteem.

By creating two giant BINGO gameboards on their classroom blackboards and attaching these desktop-published fact sheets with magnets to their magnetized blackboards, student/senior keypal team members took turns running up to cover correct answers. All the students much preferred this method of assessment to traditional tests.

Using these fact sheets, students were able to create exciting WOW—T 'N' T slide show presentations in ClarisWorks instead of writing traditional reports.

COSTS

Hardware: $400
Publishing: $200
          (Software was also donated by Claris Corporation and World Book Encyclopedia. Bell Atlantic also provided funding for this project.)

CONTACT INFORMATION

Dr. Diane S. Bloom, Administrator
Agnes Patterson Zaorski
Eatontown Public Schools: Meadowbrook/Vetter Schools
Wyckoff Road
Eatontown, NJ 07724
(732) 935-3306
(732) 542-2777
(732) 542-5046 (Fax)
e-mail: dbloom@iop.com
          AgnesZ@aol.com

Appendix A

Index by Keywords

COMPUTER CAMP

COMPUTER TECHNOLOGY

COOPERATIVE LEARNING

CRITICAL THINKING

CURRICULUM INTEGRATION

DESKTOP PUBLISHING

DISTANCE LEARNING

LANGUAGE ARTS

LAPTOP COMPUTERS

LEADERSHIP

MIDI

MILITARY

MODELING

MULTICULTURAL EDUCATION

MULTIMEDIA

MUSIC

MUSIC TECHNOLOGY

NATIONAL STANDARDS

NATURAL RESOURCES

NETWORKING

RURAL EDUCATION

SCANS COMPETENCIES

SCHOOL-TO-CAREER

SCIENCE

SCIENTIFIC INQUIRY

SENIOR CITIZENS

Simulation

SOCIAL STUDIES

STAFF DEVELOPMENT

TECHNOLOGY TRAINING

TECH PREP

TELECOMMUNICATIONS

VIDEO

WELLNESS

Appendix B

Index by Level

ELEMENTARY

MIDDLE SCHOOL

SECONDARY

K–12

Appendix C

Index by State

CALIFORNIA

COLORADO

CONNECTICUT

FLORIDA

HAWAII

IDAHO

INDIANA

KANSAS

MARYLAND

MINNESOTA

MISSISSIPPI

NEBRASKA

NEW JERSEY

NEW YORK

NORTH CAROLINA

OHIO

Appendix D

Professional Publications, Organizations, and Associations Related to Instructional Technology

PUBLICATIONS

The American Journal of Distance Education
    College of Education
    The Pennsylvania State University
    110 Rackley Building
    University Park PA 16802-3202

Educational Technology
    Educational Technology Publications, Inc.
    720 Palisades Avenue
    Englewood Cliffs, NJ 07632

Educational Technology Research and Development
    Association for Educational Communications and Technology
    1025 Vermont Ave., NW
    Suite 820
    Washington, DC 20005
    http://www.aect.org

Electronic Learning
    902 Sylvan Ave.
    Englewood Cliffs, NJ 07632

Electronic School
    National School Boards Association/Institute for the Transfer
        of Technology to Education (NSBA/ITTE)
    1680 Duke Street
    Alexandria, VA 22314-1403
    Published quarterly as a print and online supplement to *The*
        American School Board Journal
    http://www.electronic-school.com/

Florida Technology in Education Quarterly
Florida A&M University
College of Education
Tallahassee, FL 32307
http://www.famu.edu/ced/FTEQ.htm

Instruction Delivery Systems
Society for Applied Learning Technology
50 Culpepper Street
Warrenton, VA 22186

Journal of Educational Technological Systems
Society for Applied Learning Technology
50 Culpepper Street
Warrenton, VA 22186

Journal of Research on Computing in Education
International Society for Technology in Education
University of Oregon
1787 Agate Street
Eugene, OR 97403

Journal of Technology and Teacher Education
Society for Information Technology & Teacher Education
c/o AACE
PO Box 2966
Charlottesville, VA 22902

Learning and Leading with Technology
International Society for Technology in Education
University of Oregon
1787 Agate Street
Eugene, OR 97403

Media and Methods
1511 Walnut St.
Philadelphia, PA 19102

MultiMedia Schools
Information Today, Inc.
143 Old Marlton Pike
Medford, NJ 08055-8750

School Library Media Quarterly
American Library Association
American Association of School Librarians
50 E. Huron Street
Chicago, IL 60611

Technology & Learning
  Miller Freeman
  600 Harrison Street
  San Francisco, CA 94107
  http://www.techlearning.com/

Technology and Children
  International Technology Education Association
  1914 Association Drive
  Reston, VA 20191-1539
  http://www.iteawww.org

Technology Connection
  Linworth Publishing Co.
  480 East Wilson Bridge Road, Suite L
  Worthington, OH 43085
  http://www.infomall.org/Showcase/Linworth/

TechTrends: For Leaders in Education and Training
  Association for Educational Communications and Technology
  1025 Vermont Ave., NW
  Suite 820
  Washington, DC 20005

T.H.E Journal
  150 El Camino Real, Suite 112
  Tustin, CA 92780-3670
  http://www.thejournal.com

ASSOCIATIONS AND ORGANIZATIONS

American Association of School Librarians (AASL)
  50 E. Huron Street
  Chicago, IL 60611
  Publications: School Library Media Quarterly, monographs
  http://www.ala.org/aasl

Association for the Advancement of Computing in Education
  PO Box 2966
  Charlottesville, VA 22902
  http://www.aace.org

Association for Educational Communications and Technology
  (AECT)
  1025 Vermont Ave., NW
  Suite 820
  Washington, DC 20005

Publications: Educational Technology Research and Development TechTrends, monographs
Conference: Annual
http://www.aect.org

Computer Learning Foundation
PO Box 60007
Palo Alto, CA 94306
Publications: Pamphlets and monographs to support computers in schools
http://www.computerlearning.org/

Consortium for School Networking (CoSN)
PO Box 6519
Washington, DC 20035
Conference: Annual
http://cosn.org

International Society for Technology in Education (ISTE)
University of Oregon
1787 Agate Street
Eugene, OR 97403
Publications: *Learning and Leading With Technology* and the *Journal of Research on Computing in Education,* as well as eight special interest periodicals and educator-developed books and courseware
Conference: One of the sponsors of the National Educational Computing Conference (NECC) and Tel*Ed
http://www.iste.org

International Technology Education Association (ITEA)
1914 Association Drive
Reston, VA 20191-1539
Publications: *The Technology Teacher, Technology and Children, and Journal of Technology Education*
Conference: Annual
http://www.iteawww.org

National School Boards Association/Institute for the Transfer of Technology to Education (NSBA/ITTE)
1680 Duke Street
Alexandria, VA 22314-1403
Publications: Newsletter, journal, and monographs
Conference: Annual

Society for Applied Learning Technology (SALT)
    50 Culpepper Street
    Warrenton, VA 22186
    Publications: *Journal of Interactive Instructional Delivery*, instruction delivery systems, monographs
    Conferences: Meets twice/year

Society for Information Technology & Teacher Education
    c/o AACE
    PO Box 2966
    Charlottesville, VA 22902
    Publications: *Journal of Technology and Teacher Education*
    Conferences: Annual